Teaching Strategies
for
Constructivist and Developmental
Counselor Education

Teaching Strategies

for

Constructivist and Developmental
Counselor Education

Written and Edited by

**Garrett McAuliffe
and Karen Eriksen**

BERGIN & GARVEY
Westport, Connecticut • London

Library of Congress Cataloging-in-Publication Data

McAuliffe, Garrettt.
Teaching strategies for constructivist and developmental counselor education /
written and edited by Garrett McAuliffe and Karen Eriksen.
      p. cm.
   Includes bibliographical references and index.
   ISBN 0-89789-798-6 (alk. paper)
     1. Educational counseling—Study and teaching (Higher)   2. Constructivism
(Psychology)   3. Student counselors—Training of. I. Eriksen, Karen, 1956-
II. Title
LB1027.5 .M212 2002
378.1'94—dc21   2001025178

British Library Cataloguing in Publication Data is available.

Library of Congress Catalog Card Number: 2001025178
ISBN: 0-89789-798-6

First published in 2002

Bergin & Garvey, 88 Post Road West, Westport, CT 06881
An imprint of Greenwood Publishing Group, Inc.
www.greenwood.com

Printed in the United States of America

The paper used in this book complies with the
Permanent Paper Standard issued by the National
Information Standards Organization (Z39.48-1984).

P

Contents

5   **Improvisational Activities**
   Karen Eriksen, Michael O'Connor, Garrett McAuliffe

6   **In-Class Group Activities**
   Karen Eriksen, Gail Uellendahl, Joan Blacher, Garrett McAuliffe

Preface

The nature of good teaching can be elusive. Many of us associate it with dramatic performance. The chance to enthrall an involuntary audience with our wisdom and wit tempts some of us as we prepare for class. After all, we don't want our students to be bored! In that spirit, many of us who love teaching start out performing. For example, when I (Eriksen) began teaching, it was from the dual perspectives of having been an opera singer and private practice counselor. Building on those experiences, I envisioned teaching as a performance around the particular content of counseling. I immensely enjoyed teaching during that period. I was determined to be interesting, witty, insightful, and quite entertaining. At that I probably succeeded. Clearly I saw my role as much more about me and much less about my students. I heard their concerns, however: They quite rightly complained that they didn't have enough time to discuss the material together. I believe they were justified in challenging me with, "Hey, what about us? Consider what *we* need to learn and how *we* need to learn it!"

Now, a number of years of teaching have passed. I have asked for and gotten feedback. I have watched teaching role models. I have read and discussed ideas about teaching, and my perspective, thankfully, has shifted. I now realize that counseling and teaching are much more isomorphic than are opera performance and teaching. Now what engages me most is the creative work of figuring out classroom (and out of classroom) experiences that help the students to interact with the material in powerful ways. I am now enthralled by designing activities that allow them to bring the full power of their experiences, passions, and personhood into learning a profession to which they feel called. I then delight in engaging with the students in these activities, and experiencing the power of their impact on the class as a community. And finally, I thrill at watching their thinking and abilities evolve before me, knowing that I have had a role in those changes, and finding myself transformed as well.

My passion for teaching also extends to talking about it with like-minded others, as at the events that led to this book. I am enthused by exchanging ideas with other educators about how to teach, about the strategies we have designed and tried out. However, such opportunities are rare—I hear regularly from other counselor educators, and have experienced myself, how few forums exist for this type of idea exchange among college professors. Yet we had just such a forum in 1996 at the national meeting of the Association for Counselor Education and Supervision in Portland, Oregon. There, a group of counselor educators joined together to share their methods, including their "most transformative" moments in teaching, during five sessions (and ten hours) of a Teaching Methodology discussion group. The room bristled with the electricity of shared passion and enthusiasm for our common "calling."

There, the idea of continuing the dialogue in book form was born. We have had the opportunity to serve as "midwives," encouraging, coaching, cajoling, and offering feedback to our co-authors, and finally, after a nearly four-year process (a long, but necessary gestation!), joyfully giving birth.

Our initial conception became three volumes (triplets!). The earliest product, called *Preparing Counselors and Therapists: Creating Constructivist and Developmental Programs*, described foundational principles and exemplary program practices for a constructivist counselor education. It was published in the Spring of 2000 by the Association for Counselor Education and Supervision. The second, *Teaching Counselors and Therapists: Constructivist and Developmental Classroom Practices*, lines out constructivist teaching practices for the courses that make up the current canon in counselor education.

This third book, *Teaching Strategies for Constructivist and Developmental Counselor Education*, expands on the previous works by answering the sometimes urgently asked question, "But what do I do on Monday?" A "strategy" can be defined as a plan for action. The root of "strat" means "to lead" and the "eg" in the word comes from the Greek word for "act." In this book, we have generated and compiled many ways to "lead (counseling students) to action." As might be seen in Chapter One and in the cognitive psychology research (McNamara et al., 2000), "activity" (in the brain) is a necessary condition for learning. College educators often fail to instigate such activity in the "dangerously boring classrooms" of academe. This book is an invitation and a guide for us to do otherwise.

We describe in this volume both traditional and experiential strategies that instructors can use during a single class session, or in assignments that span the semester. The suggested strategies range from pointers for effective lecturing, to family sculpting, to instigation via film. In addition to explicitly describing the strategy and its developmental and constructivist foundations, each author discusses the objectives, benefits, and possible disadvantages of the activity.

We hope that reading this work stimulates you to experiment with active learning instruction and, in the process, to breathe new life into work you may have done for years. We hope that you pass along this reinvigoration of your passion to your students, inspiring them, so that, in turn, they and their counseling work are transformed. And of course, we hope further for the trickle-down effect that is most important to this entire endeavor: that the prospective clients and students of our counselors will experience the development that comes from their own transformations.

We have organized the seven segments of this book in this way: Chapter One reviews general teaching principles, outlining what we now know about good teaching from over one hundred years of research. We intend this chapter to serve as foundational reading for the many counselor educators who have received little training in teaching. Chapter Two then follows with a guide to the most effective uses of the "traditional," and most common, college teaching methods. We hope that this chapter challenges each of us to make a high craft of lecturing, leading discussions, and questioning. Chapter Three brings to the foreground the powerful personal awareness agenda that is the hallmark of counselor education, offering activities that trigger personal growth and self-awareness. In Chapter Four, we extend beyond the traditional focus on our individual experiences to highlight one of the newest thrusts of our work: increasing multicultural awareness. We have organized Chapter Five around the notion of "Improvisation," which includes any activities in which the student must generate "live" actions in class. Chapter Six illuminates the value of group work in class, using case studies, debate, and small group discussions. Finally, in Chapter Seven, we offer "projects" that stimulate students to generate and gather information from "real world" settings.

Birth cannot happen without many participants, and for those "mothers," "fathers," "grandparents," "mid-wives," and others, we give thanks. The four-year gestation period has required patience and forbearance. But the "child" has arrived, our patience and discomfort has been rewarded, and many of us have been renewed professionally partly as a result of our encounters with the other participants in this process. Now we need *you* to carry on the work, to be "the village that raises the child," to rededicate yourself to this labor of love. Perhaps you will contribute to the next edition of this ongoing story.

1

The Heart and Craft of Teaching: What We Know

Garrett McAuliffe

You probably teach very well without recognizing that, often, the more teaching, the less learning. Our job in adult education is not to cover a set of course materials, but to engage adults in effective and significant learning.
—*Jane Vella, Adult Educator*

Many counseling students leave their "training" essentially unchanged. Many are, at their epistemological core, still dutiful followers and maintainers of the status quo (Borders & Fong, 1989; Neukrug & McAuliffe, 1993). That is what drives us to embark on the risky teaching endeavors in this volume. We might all agree that counselor education is a means toward the end of "producing" empathic, enthusiastic, autonomous, and interdependent professionals. Such counselors can use the "technical" knowledge of our field selectively and artfully toward instigating changes in both individuals and systems. But what would it take for such a socially critical, self-reflective being to emerge from our programs? Is counselor education meeting the requirements of a post-modern era, one in which we honor doubt and irony as the tools for engaging a limitless diversity of ideas, norms, and cultures? Our counselor education past has given us much to build on, but too many new avenues face us in our travels for our old maps to suffice. The solid, well-trod certainties of humanism and behaviorism cannot engage this fluidity.

The tension that concerns many of us in this examination of counselor education is the sense that the pedagogical road has many forks. And while many of us aim for the destinations of multiculturalism, technical eclecticism, life span development, and the like, we are unsure of the vehicles that might carry us and our students in those directions. The "old ways" of teaching will not hold in this era. Lecture and discussion, to name the dominant teaching methods, are still useful building blocks, but not foundations. I would propose that counselor education cannot be built from any one method. Instead, like the foundations of structures in earthquake-prone regions, our pedagogy must be flexible and also strong, built to expect movement. Those "floating" foundations have many labels, among them relativism, post-modernism, social constructionism, and deconstructive thinking.

If counselors are to be prepared for the "earthquakes" of changing values, ethnicities, moral centers, gender expectations, and the like, then the designers of counselor education must prepare students (and themselves). They must "turn the world upside down"in order to relativize old verities, to, in Walt Whitman's terms, "Question everything you have learned in school, in church, or at home." And live with the uncertainty of thinking, "I might be wrong," "I might have been initiated into the wrong tribe," and "I must catch myself trying to be too complete."

Why is this flexible foundation so important? It is because lives are in our hands. And the "solid foundations" of the past have, in their certainty about the "right" procedure for teaching and counseling, been blind to their own constructedness, and have thus damaged some clients and students. Instead, our students and we, must prepare to live in a permanently vigilant state, a wary, unsettled uncertainty, while we push on to teach and to help as best we know. We must create questioners, problem-finders, counselors who are free of the habits of any one place or time.

What evidence is there for this urgency? While we do much good, it seems to be most common case schooling, including counselor education, does not "educate," in the Latin sense of leading ("ducare") students out ("e-") of familiar, habitual frames of mind. There is the case of the recent graduate counseling student of mine who declared that homosexuality in any manifestation is a simply a sin, that an inerrant source book declares it to be an "abomination," and that all efforts toward even tolerance are secular propaganda. To which a counselor educator colleague responded, in a listserv posting, "What happened during this student's undergraduate education? Aren't the liberal arts supposed to free individuals from blind adherence to inherited rules? Isn't a student supposed to arrive at the doorstep of graduate counselor education with the capacity (and inclination) to constantly seek evidence for beliefs, to question his or her own certainties, to show humane doubt and self-reflection? How can a student have graduated with a bachelor's degree with such an untested, culture-bound finality in his so-called 'thinking?'"

Perhaps this anecdote represents an aberration. However, there is strong evidence that undergraduate education does not sufficiently move students toward a relativistic epistemology (Pickering, personal communication, 2000). And graduate counselor education does not seem to affect that epistemology (Borders & Fong, 1989). Many counseling students generally seem to dwell in a vaguely subjectivist universe, one in which little is questioned as cultural artifact (Neukrug & McAuliffe, 1993).

This introductory chapter is a plea for you as a counselor educator to pay attention to student epistemology, for you to challenge students to create practice and weigh their professional decisions with considered evidence. It is also a guide to such practice. It is "liberal" education writ large that I proclaim, a subject that I have expanded on elsewhere (McAuliffe, 1999). The "liberatory" task of the counselor educator is to enhance the following habits of the mind: the ability to listen; to hear; to pause; to reflect on new phenomena; to look for evidence and counter-evidence for our views; to practice humility and self criticism; to nurture and empower the people around us; and to make and see connections among people and ideas that seem distant in time and space.

Of course, we must first ascertain, "How might we achieve those noble goals?" Therein we enter the seeming labyrinth of adult and counselor education. What do we do when? How do we know that it is good? We might wander the pedagogical landscape aimlessly, experimenting sporadically with teaching methods. Alternatively, we might navigate over the well-worn paths of teaching methods that we have found familiar and easy. Or, we can follow the third, more strenuous route: recognizing the crossroads, pondering our choices, checking out dead-ends, and asking fellow travelers for guidance. It is to this third approach that this book and this chapter are dedicated. Happily, we are not alone. One hundred years of theory and research on teaching and learning have provided us with some light and a compass for general guidance. We would be honored if we might have your company on the journey.

Some of us have been teaching for years from a fairly comatose position. Our soporific drone has covered the class with a blanket of assurance and ease—that we, the experts, will tuck the learner into a soft bed that is stuffed with knowledge. We have perhaps produced the "dangerously boring course," in Wolke's words (2000), one in which the "fragile enthusiasm of students is menaced by professors who dwell [almost exclusively] on the abstract" (p. A84). We have proclaimed as verities the principles of cognitive-behaviorism, the stages of racial identity, the nature of good tests. And our students conspire with us to stay in a "velvet rut" (Myer, 2001), a comfortable, dull place that is created by teacher-centered instruction. Students don't really like it, but they do find this passive position to be a familiar and easy, whether it be the physical comfort of the soft lecture hall seat or the mental quiescence of taking in the wisdom of the professor.

We cannot easily ignore the voices of dissent on this matter. Their clamor is everywhere. Perhaps we have heard, or even read, that the "sage on the stage" is "out" and the "guide on the side" is "in." And we may now feel badly, as Jane Tompkins, advocate of personalized, experiential college teaching, says, "My enthusiasm for the way I teach now makes some people (for example, fellow teachers) feel really badly. It seems to be saying that lecturing is no good or passe" (Schneider, 1998, p. A9).

Other educators among us have let go of this type of control. We are directors of improvisational, participatory humanistic dramas. No script is needed for the spontaneous knowledge creation of the classroom community. We flail at the desiccated academic culture that honors the head over the heart.

Thus the pendulum swings and the advocates proclaim on each side: student versus curriculum, discovery versus transmission, content versus process. And yet most of us frankly don't know what we are doing. The secret is out. College professors don't know how to teach!

Not knowing how to teach, however, is not the same as teaching poorly. As an adult educator in Chile told Jane Vella, "We have been doing this for years. We just didn't know what to call it!" (1994, p. 179). So we need not feel so badly. Surely each of us has a special knack hidden somewhere, and we use it over and over, relentlessly. We are good at test construction, role playing, story-telling, assignment-writing, Socratic questioning, or any combination of the many activities that make up the puzzle that is teaching.

And counselor education is as suspect in this regard as any field. Granello and Hazler, (1998) reviewing the writings on teaching in counselor education, found that "consistent among all authors . . . was a core belief that counselor education lacks a coherent, articulated pedagogy" (p. 89). A literature review on pedagogy in counselor education by Nelson and Neufeldt (1998) confirms that concern: The authors found no scholarly articles on the topic. Thus, while we have discussed counseling curricular content, little work has been done on how such content is best learned by students. It seems to be time for us to cross the hall and speak to our teacher preparation colleagues on method. After all, most of us are in colleges of education.

But what will we find there? Is there solid evidence of "what works in what way to produce which results, with which students," to paraphrase Williamson and Bordin's (1941) famous question about counseling research? Is there a package of the "right" teaching techniques? Of course not, as even many inveterate positivists or true-believing humanists will acknowledge. Even Jane Tompkins herself suggests, "There is no one way to teach, no single format or formula" (Schneider, 1998, p. A10). Therefore, we will honor the tentative approach to the altar of teaching and learning, but we will not be awed by the seemingly unknowable. Our only certainty might be our "en-thu-siasm" (for example, contacting our "en-theos"—"god in us") for the effort.

How do we embrace this profound endeavor despite a lack of final certainty? The teaching act is too important to dismiss. Too many lives are in our hands, both of our students and of their future clients. I propose that we, as counselor educators, devote ("vow completely"—de-votare) our-selves with this enthusiasm to the sacred charge that we have been given. In doing so we will straddle the poles of the "art vs. craft of teaching" debate. We will live with the partiality, the incompleteness of not knowing, for it is too complicated, too dialectical an enterprise for us to ever fully "know" how to teach. But we won't be over-awed either by our lack of full control over the mysteries of teaching. After all, teaching is a multivariate phenomenon that is full of interaction effects. We can fruitfully utilize the one hundred-plus years of educational theorizing and researching. We can also trust our experience and that of our colleagues. And that way lies our destination. But we must bring our hearts as well as our minds.

In this chapter, I will explore what I have framed as the "heart" of teach-ing. And then I will examine the "craft" (or "head") of teaching, digging for evidence from the rich mine of educational theory and research. The adult education literature will be our companion. So, too, will our colleagues in counselor education. And, finally, I ask you to use, for guidance, your "'N' of 1" experience as a teacher. That is only possible if you are willing to be intentionally reflective, not rote and habitual, in your work.

CONSTRUCTIVISM: A ROUTE THROUGH THE LABYRINTH

Constructivism is the guiding metaphor for this book and its compan-ion volume, *Preparing Counselors and Therapists: Creating Constructivist and Developmental Programs* (McAuliffe, Eriksen, and Associates, 2000). Constructivism is not any one method, however, although it does incline toward an inductive, active approach to teaching. It instead is a way of thinking. The general notion comes from the Piagetian developmental tra-dition of respecting the evolving meaning-making capacities of the learner. It also taps into the social constructionist impulse, in which the social/dialogical nature of human meaning-making is honored. Social construc-tionism finds its roots and its wings in the work of such thinkers as Baldwin, Mead, Hall, and, more recently, Gergen, among others. They propose that no meaning is made outside of a social context; there is no meaning "out there" to be found; we are always formed by our social context. Both "constructivisms," the developmental and the social, offer us a humbling, non-authoritarian, and open-ended understanding of human knowing.

What are the teaching implications of constructivism? Through constructivism we honor multiple perspectives, and multiple teaching methods. We honor the meaning-making capacity of every individual, through attention to such constructs as "developmental readiness" and "learning style." No longer can we live in an ordered, teacher-centered universe, surrounded by our satellite students. We pay attention to alternate paths (teaching methods) and even alternate destinations (curricular goals). Constructivist teaching is exquisitely attentive to "process:" our own, our students', and that in the classroom. Awareness of the process inevitably makes us more flexible, for that way lies attending to our own promptings (including aversions and discomforts), our students' enthusiasms and disaffections, and the crossroads (of whether to plow on, or pause and shift) that we reach in any class session. It follows that constructivism helps us to be humble, tuned in to the many and shifting voices in ourselves and in our students. Perhaps the central impulse behind constructivism is "reflexivity," a constant vigilance about one's foundations. Richard Rorty (1980), the contemporary philosopher, puts reflexivity this way, "I must consider that perhaps I have been initiated into the wrong tribe . . . ." (p. 8). That tribe might be humanism, positivism, liberation-ism, intellectualism, liberalism, right- or left-brain-ism, feminism, conservatism, and hundreds of other "true belief-isms" that the mind is heir to.

Constructivist teaching can be especially resonant for counselor educators, for such instruction mimics the act of counseling itself. Jean Peterson (personal communication, 2000), our counselor educator colleague from Purdue University, draws the parallel in this way:

> Students who have difficulty embracing [constructivist teaching] also often have difficulty going into a counseling session open to the experience of it, to the client's way of seeing the world, and to new ways of conceptualizing and strategizing. By contrast, students who begin to embrace [constructivist thinking] begin to leave 'over-preparation' behind.

With this statement, Peterson has described a hoped-for result of our work: the emergence of a theory-creating, reflexive counselor, a constructivist professional. The road to such an overarching epistemological flexibility is marked by passages, if not stumbling blocks. The developmentalists (Belinky, Clinchy, Goldberger, Tarule, 1986; Kegan, 1994, 1982; Perry, 1970) remind us—the way goes through the narrow paths marked by the rigid walls of any single-minded "method" and out into the open fields of dialogical constructivism.

A PROBLEM: DANGEROUS DUALISMS

Constructivism has sometimes been misinterpreted, I believe, as a weapon to be used against all teacher-centered instruction. We do know that the most common methods in college teaching, by a wide margin, are "class discussion" and "extensive lecturing" (Magner, 1999). Among the least–used methods are "field studies" and "group projects." What does this tell us? That we must go to war against the "teacher-centered" hegemony that puts students into a passive, receptive mode? I think not. John Dewey would ask us to examine this type of dichotomizing. He calls such factionalization, between reformers and conservatives, humanists and behaviorists, "dangerous dualisms."

Fishman and McCarthy (1998) examined Dewey's thinking on three dualisms that have predominated in the educational discourse of the last century: student and curriculum, discovery and transmission, and process and content. Dewey proposes that each side of the supposed dualism penetrates the other. Let us take an excursion, guided by Fishman and McCarthy, into Dewey's attempt to reconcile these oppositions might help us to embrace the tensions of these seeming dualisms. That way lies an integrated understanding of counselor preparation, one that might keep us as teachers and program leaders from riding the high horse for the "wrong tribe."

Living with the Tensions: Content and Process, Curriculum and Student, Transmission and Discovery

Content, transmission, curriculum. We might summarize the first side of the dichotomy as "the *content* is *transmitted* through the *curriculum* by a knowledge-giver." This supposed verity reflects standard practice in much schooling throughout history. It is grounded in an authoritarian epistemology. Kohlberg and Mayer (1972) call it the "transmission model." Freire (1970) calls it the "banking deposit" approach. Dewey calls it "penitentiary pedagogy," given its imprisonment of the learner in a classroom cell controlled by the warden-teacher. The transmission model of teaching has periodically been under attack during the past hundred years, starting with Dewey and continuing through the humanists (Lewin, 1951; Rogers, 1980), the liberationists (Freire, 1970), and the developmentalists (Kohlberg & Mayer, 1972). Dewey's notions of "interest" and "effort" as central to learning are helpful in critiquing this model. He has said that, in its extreme, the transmission approach ignores both the learners' "interest" and the necessity that the learners make an "effort" to solve problems that excite that interest. The transmission method implies that "knowers" and a "known" exist, that students are supplicants at the altar of inherited knowledge. Dewey considered such an approach to have an elitist dimension, as he saw "less competitive students yielding to boredom, losing interest, deciding they had nothing to contribute which the teacher did not already know" (Fishman & McCarthy, 1998, p. 23). Let us be wary of this side of the dualism.

Student, process, discovery. The opposite end of the continuum can be caricatured as the teacher ("facilitator") having faith that "the *student* can create knowledge exclusively through a *process of discovery.*" In its extreme, this "open" educational method has students choose content by deciding what they would like to learn. In its purest form, the "facilitator/instructor" follows student interest and merely sets up conditions for possible learning. There is no external evaluation, no standard for practice. All is creation. At its most extreme of student-centeredness, Dewey called it "sugar-coated pedagogy," for it can merely be a pleasurable indulgence in the urges of the moment, a tasting of the sweetness of whim, and a discarding of the "nutritional" wisdom of the culture. Dewey was no promoter of a simple "student-centered" pedagogy. He thought that such a self-focused romanticism left students unprepared to live in the larger community.

Dewey offers an integration of these extremes in these guidelines:

- *Student and curriculum* (including a particular lesson plan or course syllabus) must interplay. First, we must make sure that students are actively engaged in the planned curriculum. It is the teacher's task to create situations in which the student needs the curriculum and is prompted to explore, use, and remember it (Fishman & McCarthy, 1998). Thus, we use a "motivational experience," as it is often called in teacher training, for each course, each session. We bring in everyday experience through anecdotes, student journals of daily life, and video illustrations. Students thus launch themselves actively into the "problem" that the curriculum is addressing that day.

- *Transmission and discovery* are inextricable. Education has both a conserving (transmitting) and a reforming (discovering) function. It conserves by recognizing that a culture consists of shared stories, a community with common history and allegiances. We thus must still "transmit"—even with a healthy skepticism for the culture- and time-boundedness of all knowledge—the best thinking and doing of past generations. The problem for Dewey with the transmission approach to schooling is the direct way in which a culture tries to pass these stories on to students, forgets the fact that what is being transmitted was once itself created in a context and revised in light of new discoveries. Direct transmission ignores differing individual interests and capacities. Instead, while learners do build on the past, they sometimes overturn its "truths" when their inquiring minds make new discoveries.

- *Content and process* can also be set up in opposition, creating another dangerous dualism. We need to attend to the learning process itself, not just to the content (they are inseparable, according to Dewey). Content has always been generated through a discovery process. Cultures that have adapted well have allowed newness into their environments. The content of education is often the process itself—learning to hypothesize, search for evidence, question assumptions, consider multiple possibilities, and consult with other knowers. We can replicate that "process" in the classroom. Dewey would remind us that knowledge is not an ownable "content," a reifiable attribute, but a charged activity, a way that people make connections with their surroundings. It comes from habits of mind—habits that he calls "reflection" and "intelligence" (Fishman & McCarthy, 1998, p. 25). This is the content-process nexus.

Let us heed Dewey's warning about dualisms as we explore the possibilities for a more intentional pedagogy in counselor education. Let us "catch ourselves trying to be too complete," in Kegan's words. Let us be self-critical of our allegiances. Let us make room for all voices, for the greatest danger is silence.

The following is a division of effective teaching, into two dimensions: the "heart" and the "craft." The distinction builds on Dewey's and other thinkers' work. I hope that these distinctions are helpful but not seductive, given both the limits and the power of language and of the human mind's ineluctable tendency to categorize. "Heart" and "craft" vaguely parallel Bloom's (1956) "affective" and "cognitive" domains.

THE "HEART" OF TEACHING: EMOTION, EXPERIENCE, AND MORAL PURPOSE

> *Heart:* a. Emotional constitution, basic disposition, or character. b. One's prevailing mood or current inclination. c. Capacity for sympathy or generosity; compassion. d. Love; affection. e. Courage; resolution; fortitude.
> —*The American Heritage Dictionary of the English Language*

The Role of the Emotions in Learning

Learning is an emotionally charged activity. Stephen Fishman, in his exposition of Dewey's thoughts on teaching, states it in this way: "Learning occurs when desire is frustrated, attention is aroused, and we investigate our surroundings with a purpose, learning new ways to achieve our sought-after ends" (Fishman & McCarthy, 1998, p. 19). Emotional arousal is a condition for learning in everyday life. The Root-Bernsteins (2000) remark on the creative methods of literary artists and scientists: Such thinkers begin first with a pre-verbal "apprehension" (as an "intimation" might alert a counselor to a potentially important issue in a session). Bertrand Russell, the philosopher, for instance, claimed that he first noted a "feeling of discomfort" as the recognition of a problem to be solved. Next he had a willingness to operate with non-symbolic senses and emotions. Finally, he translated these "ideas" into a conventional symbolic form. Einstein reported similarly that he conducted "mental experiments involving visual images and muscular feelings" and then translated them into words or other symbols (Root-Bernstein, 2000).

Thus we might conclude that we do our most creative thinking when we begin with strong emotion. The counseling professional who can "hear," or "see," or "feel" a problem, and can create interventions with individuals and in systems by pausing, accessing images and intuitions, and then expressing possibilities, brings insights beyond those available only through "technique" or craft, to use my current terminology. The Root-Bernsteins advise teachers to create opportunities for students to "feel" issues through classroom dramas, visual sculpting, drawing, and other pre-verbal sense-making experiences in order to energize their inventive capacities.

Emotion also powerfully contributes to remembering, as the famous hot stove example in childhood reminds us. McNamara, Scott, and Bess (2000) also cite the evidence for the role of emotion in learning. So, let us trigger emotional moments in our teaching. But, let us be warned: The emotions alone do not result in useful knowledge. David Kolb's (1984) work provides a model for the interplay of feeling and thought, experience and reflection, the concrete and the abstract, in learning.

Experience and the Learning Cycle

In Kolb's "experiential learning" cycle (Kolb, 1984), both sensory and verbal modes of thinking are honored; that is, concrete experiencing, reflecting and observing, abstract conceptualizing, and active experimenting (or "applying"). Counselor educators wisely consider all of these modes in their instructional design. All of them matter.

The first and last of Kolb's domains (experiencing and experimenting) are least present in most college classrooms (Magner, 2000). College teaching, and even counselor education, are dominated by the middle two: reflection (through discussion, questioning, journaling) and abstraction (often through lecture, papers, and projects). Ironically, Kolb's research indicates that counselors and other mental health professionals prefer the oppositeexperiencing and applying! My own research on counseling students (McAuliffe, 2000) confirms Kolb's findings, as students reported "experience" and "positive affect" to be among the most powerful influences on their development as aspiring counselors.

Should we, therefore, "drop everything" and rush to the experiential education camp? Of course not, as Kolb (and Dewey) would remind us. Balance is needed, as is attention to individual learning style preferences. But, given the relative absence of experiential teaching in higher education and the preference for it among students of counseling, we might take bold steps in that direction.

There is one proviso, however: Let us not cast aside the power of the abstraction, the generalizations that help us leave the ground of the concrete. For experience and experimentation to move from specific, undifferentiated "learning" to generalizable "knowledge," they must be tested in the forge of logic, experiment, and dialogue. And there the academy already shines. It is therefore not "mere" experience that is the best teacher. It is the *cycle* of experience, reflection, abstraction, and experimentation that wins the day. The lesson of Kolb's learning cycle for counselor-educators is to "Mix your methods." Chickering and Reisser (1993) concur, suggesting that we use "the junkyard curriculum." That is, since it is not possible to completely individualize our teaching, we must select varied elements from our whole collection of teaching methods. Lest we end on a note of wanton multiplicity, however, we might derive a few specific counselor education practices and reminders from Kolb's work:

- Remember that counseling students tend to be inclined more toward experience and application than toward reflection and abstraction. All are important.

- Sequence the learning modes in a course. For example, instructors might follow Kolb's learning cycle in an "Introduction to Counseling" course in the following way:

  Experiencing. Students shadow practicing counselors for a series of sessions.

  Examining. During and between observations, they note their feelings and thoughts while on site and categorize their observations.

  Explaining. The whole class pools their results and generates a model of what they have observed, perhaps entitled "the purposes, functions, and problems of a school counselor."

  Applying. Students return to interview and further observe counselors, applying their "explanations." Students then refine their initial explanation.

- Sequence the whole master's curriculum to incorporate experience. Such an experientially-based counselor education might consist of the following sequence:

  1). Students begin their studies with a heavy dose of experience, beginning a semester or course in the field, combined with class discussions about the experiences (for example, a fieldwork-grounded Introduction to Counseling course and an experientially-oriented Helping Interview course, each with an emphasis on concrete experience and reflective observation).

2). They tie the experiences to the conceptual framework of the discipline, via the readings and discussions (such as courses as Counseling Theories, Life span Development, and Diagnosis and Treatment Planning).

3). Students work both as teams and individually to construct uses for the theories (for example, via simulations, group projects, role playing; in such courses as Testing, Career Counseling, Addictions, Group Work, Family Counseling, and Counseling Practices in Schools, Agencies, and / or Colleges).

4). They would go back into the field to try out these applications.

• *Mix modes and activities.* The seeming rigidity of such a linear or even cyclical approach to learning must, of course, be modified by the spontaneities, diversities, opportunities, and constrictions of our educational environments. For example, a video presentation might serve as an "experience," an "explanation," or both of counseling (cf. the "Gloria" demonstrations and subsequent presentations by therapists). Similarly, a discussion can be used to "examine" (reflect on) experience or to "explain" abstractions in class.

Emotion Meets Experience

Experience, with its attendant emotional arousal, is both the spark that lights the lamp of learning and the oil that burns it into memory. It both motivates and contributes to retention. If we remember that in all environments, both school and non-school (in counseling), learning occurs in the emotional moments when the individual and the environment clash, then we as teachers might help learners to be "always active" (a key word for Dewey). For Dewey, knowledge must be constructed by the learner in the laboratory of experience and tested in the fire of experience. Dewey is adamant: "There can be no effective school learning . . . without the learner's active participation" (Fishman & McCarthy, p. 20). Teachers must instigate such arousal.

Emotion also helps us to persist. In the "dangerously boring course" (Wolke, 2000), students dismiss original thought in favor of a construct-maintaining passivity. Instead, Dewey proposes that the educator help students identify goals for learning, or "for-whats," in Dewey's language. Dewey proposes that students be "intent on something urgent" (Fishman & McCarthy, 1998, p. 19). Learning-triggering arousal occurs when students see continuities between their current lives, their schoolwork, and their futures. Dewey suggests that the emotion behind the "for what's" sustains us in the midst of difficult moments in learning. He continues,

"When our objectives are road-blocked, emotions like joy and fear, and dispositions like persistence and initiative, sustain the thinking . . . ." In counselor education, such interest-sustaining motivators might include reminders of the impact of counseling, the nature of particular social problems, and the value of course content for actual practice.

Moral Purpose

One of the "for-whats" of education, for Dewey, is passionate engagement in moral action. The educational enterprise is ultimately moral; it is dedicated to the welfare of the human community. His vision might be a beacon for counselor education. Dewey urges educators to aim relentlessly at students' developing "traits of character," which he believes supercede mere cognitive intelligence or the ability to think logically. He proposes that our ultimate purposes in education are to "promote cooperative living," "to advance community welfare," and "to improve the condition of others." Dewey again emphasizes thinking as central to moral education. In order to guard against "fundamentalisms," or morals being only "mores" (inherited cultural norms), that can lead to the hegemony of the powerful and/or the majority. He says that students must have opportunities to make choices, not to merely accept beliefs blindly on the basis of authority, fancy, or superstition. We might translate that distinction as a proposal that all education be aimed at instigating movement toward Kohlberg's post-conventional thinking and away from norm-dependent thinking. Dewey takes procedural knowing a step further, toward "moral action" (Rest, 1995) in his urging that students develop the inclination to scrutinize accepted language, practice, and belief. That inclination might occur partly through experiencing a classroom atmosphere that is consistently dialogical, egalitarian, and reflective. (A good example of the process being indistinguishable from the content.) He reminds us not to allow seemingly subordinate ends, such as papers and grades, to be privileged over the more ultimate ends of care, a socially critical stance, and moral action.

In this morally alert vein, counselor educators might ask themselves: "Can I stand at graduation or at the end of a course, and say that I have made a continuing effort to help students develop, above all else, in Dewey's words, 'the will for cooperation and the heart which sees in every other individual one who has an equal right to share in the cultural and material fruits of collective human invention'?" (Fishman & McCarthy, 1998, p. 48).

Many of us lose sight of the moral purpose. I once asked a small sample of counselor educators, "Why do you do this work?" I received the following responses: "To be in an academic atmosphere," "To establish a strong reputation," "To write well-known books," "To have a flexible work environment," "To do what I love: train," and "To use my teaching skills." From no one did I hear a more ultimate purpose (although it may have been implicit). Their "vision of the work," in Kegan's terms, did not include a socially critical, post-conventional dimension. How are we then to instigate such thinking in students?

In contrast, on a recent visit to a religiously affiliated university, I was struck by the consistent moral purpose that pervaded the counselor education program. Students and professors spoke of the "service" dimension of counseling." They enacted that purpose through service projects, as moral discussions on-campus reminders, and in-class discussion of the ultimate ends of our work.

I am reminded by these previous two contrasting experiences of how easy it is to become a technician, or even a technology-creator, in the secular university of this era. Perhaps we have allowed the political and media demagogues, the television preachers, to take the moral center stage. Perhaps we teach, for instance, Rogers' methods without Rogers' moral and political vision. It is significant that many of the leading counseling theorists considered moral issues to be the centerpiece of their work. They were themselves moral thinkers, clergy, or offspring of clergy, including Rogers, Bolles, Ellis, Jung, Wrenn, and Frankl.

Yes, the great reach of the modern era for a rational, rather than superstitious, ground for knowledge is noble. Its pursuit has, however, left many of us to be "trainers" rather than "educators." We do not "lead students out" (e-ducare) of familiar, habitual ways of knowing. We are often functionaries in programs without a moral center.

Jane Addams, the social reformer and friend of John Dewey's, offers us guidance in this regard from one hundred years ago: "We recall that the first colleges . . . were established to educate religious teachers . . . . As the college changed from teaching theology to teaching secular knowledge, the test of its success should have shifted from the power to save [people's] souls to the power to adjust them in healthful relations to nature and their fellow men. But the college failed to do this, and made the test of its success the mere collecting and disseminating of knowledge, elevating the means into an end and falling in love with its own achievements" (Addams, 1994).

I suspect that we need to remind ourselves of our initial vision for this work. We might also challenge ourselves to use Kegan's "self-authorizing" capacity (which most of us can at least apprehend from our conventional perch) to define a moral purpose for our work as counselor educators, to renew that initial commitment, and to find ways to enact it further. And we must dedicate ourselves to communicating this moral purpose in our classes. We can especially do so in the following setting: new student orientation, introductory class (professional purposes), social and cultural issues course (disparity), career course (access and opportunity), skills class (expressed empathy as a moral action), fieldwork seminars (ethical imperatives), and the "practices of school/agency/student affairs" courses (prevention, institutional inequalities). Counselor education is a way of living, as well as a way of working, after all. Once we return to that center, we can go back to trigger the "open-mindedness," "wholeheartedness," and "responsibility" in students that Dewey cared so much about.

Suggestions for Engaging the Heart in Teaching

Given the power of affect in learning, what are concrete practices that might incorporate the "heart?" Jane Vella (1994), the international adult educator, has enumerated twelve "principles for effective adult learning." Among these are four that I would deem "affective," in that they attend to the emotional and attitudinal domains. If they are heeded, I believe that future counselors would more likely become moral agents in the profession, especially through watching their teachers in action.

Create a feeling of safety. We have all known fear in the classroom—like all emotionally-laden learning, we cannot forget it. I know it from my first day in second grade when I was marched to the board in front of the class to demonstrate the multiplication that I had forgotten over the long, dreamy summer! My potential was not affirmed that day; my profligacy was. As I stood at the board I quaked at the teacher's imminent condemnation of my blissful ignorance and self-indulgent vacation. I still smell the chalk, hear the buzz of my peers, feel the arched brows of Sister Philomena, see her hulking black-and-white shadow over me in my small blue suit. Such impressions travel right through the senses to land in permanent memory.

The emotions that I experienced on that day resulted in a rich long-term memory of the situation, but they were not helpful for me as a growing person. Learners instead need affirmation of their potential and their achievements. They need to believe that this experience will work for them, that the conditions are set up for their success. How might we consistently create such an expectation of success? Not by reducing the challenge to students and the effort expected. No, that would surely be the "sugar-coated pedagogy" that Dewey feared. Safety can still be maintained even in the company of demanding challenges. Vella proposes the following specific ways to create safety:

- Help students gain confidence in course design and in the teacher by making that design and the requirements clear and by sharing your background and passion for the subject. When we ourselves are not comfortable with our knowledge, either of the process or the content, we retreat into obfuscation and posing.

- Ask learners about their expectations for the course; ask them what norms they would like, for breaks, "air time," respect, etc.

- Ensure that the course objectives are feasible; tell students how they were developed (for example, through a needs assessment of what learners need in this topic area); make the objectives flexible, based on the group's needs; start simple and build to greater complexity in tasks and topics.

- Be nonjudgmental and affirming; acknowledge each student offering, whether verbal or written, in some way; students will then use the power they already have to increase their spontaneous contributions.

Ensure the existence of sound relationships. Counselor education can be viewed as a dialogue between adult women and men who see themselves as peers. The relationship between student and teacher stands out above all other factors in research on the effects of adult literacy education (Vella, 1994). I have tried to show interest in and engagement with students as fellow persons by sending a pre-course e-mail communication to them. At that time I send a warm welcoming message, accompanied by the syllabus. Such relational connections (as opposed to purely task-oriented communications) establish the students as subjects of their own learning, not as objects. We need to show interest in students' perspectives, and assess their expectations, needs, and experiences in an ongoing way. Overall, we need to make the relationship at least equal to the task by showing interest, being humble, listening, and demonstrating respect. I personally have to remind myself of the importance of treating the students as "subjects" when I am challenged on a grade. I must open myself, both physically (in terms of my body language) and emotionally, through my reminding myself of the importance of the issue to the student and his or her right to inquire about it. My automatic response, in contrast, is often to be defensive and then elusive. Here are some specific suggestions for ensuring sound relationships:

- Use names in addressing students.

- Offer access to you (via e-mail and phone).

- Invite questions.

- Explain your rationales for activities and assignments.

- Challenge your initial or ongoing prejudices, find a place in yourself to respect each learner, even when you take a disliking for a student.

Show respect for learners as agents. More than warmth and personal relationships with students is required for counseling students to learn *for themselves.* When we ask adult students what and how they would like to learn, they subsequently become engaged and intentional (Dewey's "for-what" is ensured). As in counseling, counselor educators don't "do" for the learner what she or he can do for her or himself. Much learning occurs in the deciding on the activities and topics themselves. Engaging learners in such decision making may radically change our way of teaching. I remember well in my second year of university teaching when a student, fresh out of an adult education theory course, shocked me with the request, "Can we design the course together, as adult learners?" Today I typically offer opportunities for students to reconstruct the syllabus. Some specific "respectful" reminders are:

- Treat adult students as capable of making decisions in the course, just as they do in the other parts of their lives.

- Consider teacher-student dialogue as between "two adult subjects."

- Ask students for their views, their suggestions, their answers.

- Make the course content and process an "open system" - subject to student affirmations, additions, and critiques.

- Clarify when students are to be "consultants" who are making suggestions and when they are "deliberators" who are making decisions; allow the latter as much as possible.

Engage learners. My colleagues and I recently ran two large conferences for school personnel on working with troubled youth. One of the daylong conferences was presentation-focused, with so-called "experts" telling audiences about promising practices. The second conference was participation-oriented, with attendees creating much of the content in small discussion groups. It was very clear that the latter approach was preferred. Out of that engaged session came action plans and fervent dedication to implementing new practices for reaching troubled youth in schools. I will remind myself of this powerful difference whenever I am tempted to deliver content instead of evoking it, to tell instead of asking. Jane Vella suggests that educators engage learners by setting up tasks that invite them often to "get into it deeply," in groups. We will know that we have engaged them when it becomes difficult to stop the "buzz" of discussion! Here are some reminders:

- Involve learners emotionally via activity, make it difficult for them to extricate themselves!

- Treat a learning task as an open question put to a small group, providing the materials and resources needed to respond.

- Be wary of merely "covering" a set curriculum; you may cover all of the supposed content, but what have students learned for use? Have they been superficially covered, as by a thin blanket that can't be used outside of bed? Or, have they dressed themselves in the layers they need for many situations, leaving out superfluous materials?

THE CRAFT OF TEACHING

We now turn to seven reminders for "crafting" teaching. To separate the "heart" from the craft of teaching is to court another dangerous dualism. While the brain does have separate regions for emotional and cognitive processing, this distinction might do disservice to the intersection of heart and craft, content and process, innovation and conservation in teaching practice. But for the sake of the current task, I will maintain these metaphors.

Principles for Effective Adult Education

We again turn to adult educator Jane Vella (1994) for guidance. Among her "principles for effective adult education" are seven that speak directly to the craft of teaching. They are consistent with a constructivist educational impulse.

Do needs assessments. Counseling students, like all learners, come to us with much prior experience and with considerable knowledge. If our work is to acknowledge social construction, and if it is to be socially critical (Giroux, 1992), including all of those who are affected by the educational enterprise, then it is important to ask, "Who needs what, as defined by whom?" before we deign to deliver our approximation of what we think students need.

We might therefore ask two questions of students, in varying forms: "What do you think you need to know?" and "What do you already know?" We can make such assessments in more or less formal ways: via an open-ended verbal exchange, by means of anonymous written statements, and through a pre-written checklist of possible student needs. A developmental method of assessing students' epistemological needs consists of determining their current cognitive capacity via one of the standardized cognitive developmental measures (Moore, 1987) and tailor instruction to students' readiness.

We can also ask students about their learning needs throughout a course, especially at the beginning. The difficulty inherent in asking such questions is that adult students will answer us! That may not be comfortable. We then face decisions about how or how not to adjust our instructional designs. That tension must be endured, however, if we are to engage in the dialectic of constructivist teaching. I have found that it is helpful to offer the students a "menu" of two to four possible topics and/or classroom processes for a particular class session. With this needs-responsive method, I let go of more rigid "lesson plans." We might also store up student suggestions for future consideration. I have collected such suggestions by having students send me their responses to class sessions via e-mail, expressing their preferences for the sessions to follow. I often then read such suggestions publicly in order to check out their generalizability to and urgency for other class members.

Provide sequence and reinforcement. Instructional consultants usually repeat the mantra, "Keep it simple." Most of the issues in counseling are not simple, however. Thus we face the dilemma – how might we instigate useful, complex learning in a way that is accessible? All learners benefit from hearing the elegant simplicity of one idea, one theory, one method, before they are asked to compare, contrast, and/or integrate. Start with simple, safe tasks. Take small steps between tasks. Repeat facts, skills, and attitudes in new and interesting ways during a course or throughout a curriculum (often called the "spiral curriculum" because of the way that instructors return to simple ideas in more complex ways as students move through a program of study). Let students experience practical results from trying out their ideas. Knefelkamp (1984) described the centrality of such simple-to-complex movement in her work on developmental instruction. If we "flit" from abstract concept to concept, failing to help students see foundations and applications, or if we bombard them with intricate explanations and exceptions, we will pay the price of students' self-doubt about their capacities as learners and/or future professionals. They will rarely tell us so, however. They will instead fade and drop out.

Emphasize praxis. "Praxis" is the ancient Greek word that means "action with reflection." I have reviewed Kolb's experiential learning theory earlier in this chapter. Vella reminds us that the "doing-and-reflection dance" is a two-step: Through praxis, we mimic how we learn in everyday life, as Dewey has iterated: We act, we reflect on implications, and we then (sometimes) change our approach to a more adaptive one. Kolb offers us a slightly different language for this cycle. He describes a cyclical movement from activity, to reflection, to new activity, to conceptualization, returning again to application.

To enact praxis in a class session on human development or counseling theories, for example, we can begin by having students read cases and then pull out developmental issues or theoretical implications. Or, in an assessment course, students might take and interpret a test and then be asked, "How did you use the concept of 'norm' in this interpretation?" Students in a social and cultural issues course might apply the topics by pondering when they themselves have experienced stereotyping and what that experience was like.

I find these examples to be almost too obvious to mention. Except that I still, like many of you, have a tendency to over-abstract, leaving students behind in my enthusiasm for airy conceptual thinking. To counter such an inclination, I must repeat the mantra that Dewey calls the "so what?" dimension of learning: "Have students identify genuine problems and use the curriculum to investigate and discover solutions to these problems." We must ask ourselves: How do I instigate (or capitalize on already existing) "for whats," or needs-to-know, in students?

Provide opportunities for immediate application. We, counselors and counselor educators, are a practical people. We of necessity, or by inclination, temporarily set aside the theorizing of the social sciences and the humanities in order to do good in the world in direct ways. This is just as true of our adult students. They have multiple life roles; time is limited; they are not "captured" in a semi-suspended state as are traditional-aged residential undergraduates. Therefore, we need to help them to experience the immediate usefulness of their learning. We need to clothe the dry bones of theory with flesh. Students need to leave a class session with a skill to practice an application to make. Have them diagnose themselves, test themselves, do a diversity assessment on themselves and their neighbors. Have them observe "identity confusion" or "industry versus inferiority" in individuals and hypothesize about interventions that might assist in such crises. They need to take concepts home.

Practice equity. One of our goals is to empower students to become "actors" in the extemporaneous drama of the human community. Yet we have inherited, in Vella's words, "ancient hierarchical relationships" from our own schooling experiences. Aristocracies of age, gender, and title have preceded us. We cannot "infantilize" adult students by maintaining rigid hierarchical relationships at the same time as we attempt to help them to become autonomous-thinking professionals. If we do so, we risk intimidating students and assigning them to second-class status in the academy and the profession. Don't do it. To paraphrase the Zen expression, help them to "kill" the professor. Or, in Christian terms, wash their feet . . . practice humility.

Vella describes the alternative: "Adults need reinforcement of the human equity between teacher and student" (1994, p. 17). We can promote equity and empowerment by acknowledging the inherited hierarchies, the normative rules and roles. Then we can deconstruct them and reinvent an order that acknowledges the essential equality of all human beings.

Here is a litany of possible practices that promote equity: Try using first names, sitting within the circle of learners. Show doubt (Freire, 1990; hooks, 1994; Schniedewind, 1987). Show your "warts." Self-disclose. Laugh at yourself. Make out-of-class contact with students. Bring them to conferences, present with them. Meet them at dinners and parties and student organization gatherings. Listen to Vella: "Time spent with learners...in a different role makes a big difference in their freedom to ask the disturbing question, to disagree with a point, to venture a novel opinion" (1994, p. 18). Only with a fundamental equity in place is dialogue possible.

Encourage teamwork. Groups are a constant in our work and in much of the rest of our lives. When in a group, we are not in an "ivory tower," we are in the "real world." Our interactions are grounded in the stuff of daily interaction—forays into certainty, retreats into doubt, variations in relative contribution, adjustments in the face of conflict, attempts at openness with others, and defenses in the face of threat. Freire (1990) calls groups "limit situations" in that they reflect our imperfect worlds, more so than does the "purity" of a well-delivered lecture or a rarified discussion. Students can experience the inevitability of limit situations by working in teams.

When we ask students to participate on a team for a discussion or a project, we parallel the professional world of organizations. We also enact the community creation of knowledge. Classroom teams can focus on producing a tangible product or solution. To accomplish this end, members must propose and retreat, weigh and declaim, feel and avoid, as do participants in any project, whether they be the founders of a republic who are penning a declaration of independence or colleagues who are drafting an individualized educational plan in a school. Vella offers some guidelines for teaching using teams of adults:

- Having students work in small group teams does not require that there be a small class; teams can be formed within a group of hundreds.

- Consider how to form teams: letting them form their own groups expresses respect for their capacities to find compatible partners; forming teams for the class usually creates greater diversity and challenges students to move out of their personal and cultural "comfort zones."

- Direct the teams toward a learning task, whether it be creating a list of ideas on newsprint or developing a simulated community agency.

- Have learners pay attention to the *process* as well as the *product*:

  1). Invite learners to examine their roles on a team; start with having them assess their usual roles (for example, relationship maintenance, task achievement)

  2). Ask learners to assess formatively and summatively; that is, have them comment during and at the end of the project via journal entries, a structured questionnaire, or a commentary that is added to the final product on how they are working pr have worked.

Practice accountability. Another humility-requiring-but-democratic impulse is being accountable to our students. Formative evaluations allow adult learners to participate weekly or regularly in their learning and give the instructor a means of taking the classroom "temperature." At the end of class sessions, instructors might take five minutes to ask: "What was most useful for you today?" and "What might be changed for next time?" Summative evaluations offer students a chance to voice their accomplishments and to name what is still to be done at another time.

The principle of "accountability to the learners" also asks us to make learning goals explicit and to provide means of letting students know when they have learned them (and when not). It would be good to give students opportunities to show their competence *in situ* by, for example, leading a group, consulting on a psychological test, conducting a career decision-making session, or interviewing individuals who are markedly culturally different from themselves. By testing "learnings" in the fire of experience, students can hold us accountable as teachers.

CONCLUSION

If our students are to engage other inhabitants of our so-called postmodern world of fluid norms and surprising juxtapositions, they must be prepared with a corresponding epistemology. Yes, we can pass on the best that has been developed in our cultures. But it is through construction—letting students become shoulder-to-shoulder colleagues with us, midwives who preside at the birth of ideas that we prepare them to make the world a more humane place. As co-constructors, students can become free of habitual frames of mind and inherited hierarchies of status. We must invite them into the universal circle of knowledge-creators, let them in on our doubt, create conditions for their synapses to be charged with discovery. This work of constructing the profession is hard and ongoing. No rest is possible. Only when we engage in such work, can we march with the generations of "freedom fighters," the toilers in the factory of human community, the Voltaires, the Paines, the Rushdies, the Joyces, the Chopins, the Addamses, the Deweys, and Rogerses, to name a few. They are the ones who have pried open the doors of habit and hierarchy to let us all in as makers and remakers of this most moral of endeavors, the work of counseling.

REFERENCES

Addams, J. (1994). A function of the social settlement. In E. C. Lagemann, *On education*, (pp. 76-95). New Brunswick, NJ: Transaction Publishers.

Belenky, M., Clinchy, B., Goldberger, N., & Tarule, J. (1986). *Women's ways of knowing*. New York: Basic Books.

Bloom, B. S. (1956). *A taxonomy of educational objectives*. New York: Longman.

Borders, L. D, & Fong, M L. (1989). Ego development and counseling ability during training. *Counselor Education and Supervision, 29,* 71-83.

Chickering, A., & Reisser, L. (1993). *Education and identity* (2nd ed.). San Francisco: Jossey Bass.

Dewey, J. (1938). *Experience and education*. New York: Collier.

Fishman, S. M., & McCarthy, L. (1998). *John Dewey and the challenge of classroom practice*. New York: Teachers College Press.

Freire, P. (1970). *Pedagogy of the oppressed*. New York: Continuum.

Giroux, H. (1992). *Border crossings: Cultural workers and the politics of education*. New York: Routledge.

Granello, D. H., & Hazler, R. J. (1998). A developmental rationale for curriculum order and teaching styles in counselor education programs. *Counselor Education and Supervision, 38,* 89-105.

hooks, b. (1994). *Teaching to transgress*. New York: Routledge.

Kegan, R. (1994). *In over our heads: The mental demands of modern life*. Cambridge: Harvard University Press.

Knefelkamp, L. (1984). Developmental instruction. In L. L. Knefelkamp & R. R. Golec (Eds.), *A workbook for using the P-T-P Model,* (pp. 29-35). Unpublished document developed for use in the University of Maryland Counseling and Personnel Services Department.

Kohlberg, L., & Mayer, R. (1972). Development as the aim of education. *Harvard Educational Review, 42,* 449-496.

Kolb, D. (1984). *Experiential learning: Experience as the source of learning and development*. Englewood Cliffs, NJ: Prentice Hall.

Lewin, K. (1951). *Field theory in social science*. New York: HarperCollins.

Magner, D. K. (September 8, 1999). The graying professoriate. *The Chronicle of Higher Education,* A18-19.

McAuliffe, G. J. (Summer 1999). Is there a liberal bias in multicultural counselor education? Becoming a "multicultural liberal." *ACES Spectrum,* p. 9.

McAuliffe, G. J. (2000). How counselor education influences future helpers: What students say. In G. McAuliffe, K. Eriksen & Associates, *Preparing counselors and therapists: Creating constructivist and developmental programs* (pp. 42-61). Alexandria, VA: Association for Counselor Education and Supervision.

McAuliffe, G., Eriksen, K., & Associates (2000). *Preparing counselors and therapists: Creating constructivist and developmental programs*. Alexandria, VA: Association for Counselor Education and Supervision.

McNamara, D. S., Scott, J., & Bess, T. (2000). Building blocks of knowledge: Cognitive foundations for constructivist counselor education. In G. McAuliffe, K. Eriksen, and Associates, *Preparing counselors and therapists: Creating constructivist and developmental programs* (pp. 62-76). Alexandria, VA: Association for Counselor Education and Supervision.

Moore, W. S. (1987). The Learning Environment Preferences: Establishing preliminary reliability and validity for an objective measure of the Perry scheme of intellectual development. *Dissertation Abstracts International*, 8808586.

Myer, R. (2001). Community agency counseling: Teaching about management and administration. In K. Eriksen, and G. McAuliffe, Eds., *Teaching counselors and therapists* (pp. 255-266). Westport, CT: Bergin & Garvey.

Nelson, M. L., & Neufeldt, S. A. (1998). The pedagogy of counseling: A critical examination. *Counselor Education and Supervision, 38,* 70-88.

Neukrug, E. S., & McAuliffe, G. J. (1993). Cognitive development and human service education. *Human Service Education, 13,* 13-26.

Perry, W. G. (1970). *Forms of intellectual and ethical development in the college years.* New York: Holt, Rinehart, & Winston.

Rest, J. (1995). Notes for an aspiring researcher in moral development theory and practice. *Moral Education Forum, 20,* 11-14.

Rogers, C. R. (1980). *Freedom to learn for the 80's.* Columbus, OH: Merrill.

Root-Bernstein, R.S., & Root-Bernstein, M. (2000). Learning to think with emotion. *The chronicle of Higher Education.* Jan. 14, 2000, A64.

Rorty, R. (1989). *Contingency, irony, and solidarity.* New York: Cambridge University Press.

Schneider, A. (1998). Jane Tompkins' message to academe: Nurture the individual, not just the intellect. *Chronicle of Higher Education, 44,* A8-A10.

Schniedewind, N. (1987) Feminist values: Guidelines for teaching methodology in women's studies. In I. Shor (Ed.), *Freire for the classroom,* (pp. 170-179). New York: Boynton/Cook.

Vella, J. (1994). *Learning to listen, learning to teach: The power of dialogue in educating adults.* San Francisco: Jossey-Bass.

Williamson, E. G., & Bordin, E. S. (1941). The evaluation of educational and vocational counseling: A critique of methodology of experiments. *Educational Psychology and Psychological Measurement, 1,* 5-24.

Wolke, R. L. (2000, January 16). Dangerously boring courses. *Chronicle of Higher Education,* A84.

2

Using Traditional Teaching Methods Effectively: A Guide to Lecturing, Asking Questions, and Leading Discussions

Garrett McAuliffe

"But what do I do on Monday?" ask the teachers who gather at education conferences. I first heard it when I myself labored in the junior high and elementary school teaching fields of New York in the 1970s. We now know enough about what works in teaching answer them: be flexible, emphasize experience, use multiple methods. But many of us will continue to rely on the traditional virtue of lecturing, questioning, and discussion-leading. If these are our modes, let us do them well. Let us listen to the research on what works in teaching.

That is what Freiberg and Driscoll (1996) have done in laying out so-called "universal teaching strategies." I will use their description of what works as a springboard for the following presentation of largely research-based practices in lecturing, questioning, and discussion-leading that have shown superiority over other methods. So, college professor, here is your initiation into the secrets of good teaching, verities that your public school counterparts learned, perhaps while you were writing your dissertation. While I will treat these three strategies separately, they can and should be thoughtfully combined in teaching practice.

LECTURE

"Horrors! Lecture?" I hear from the humanistic and constructivist educators among you. "The lecture is dead. The 'the sage on the stage' has been dismissed in favor of 'the guide on the side.'" And, "How can a teacher-centered method like lecturing ever fit in a book dedicated to constructivism?"

Perhaps we have misunderstood constructivism. It has broad shoulders. Constructivism carries many methods, as long as they are guided by attention to individual readinesses and styles, and openness to dialogue and equality among learners. Lecture, thoughtfully designed and integrated into teaching, can therefore be part of the construction. There must be, after all, reasons why lecture remains one of the most common teaching methods at universities. So, let us not become polarized and dualistic. But let us lecture well, if we are to do it.

Lecture must be organized, focused, varied, and deliberate in order to stimulate understanding for most students. I suspect that most of us will bring one or two of these qualities to our lectures, but not all. So—here are some pointers for lecturing, as drawn from Freiberg and Driscoll's delineation of research-demonstrated teaching strategies. First, decide if lecture is the best way to achieve the learning goal.

- *Reasons to choose lecture.* Lecture can serve at least three purposes: (1) to provide information, (2) to motivate, even inspire, a group, and (3) to stimulate critical thinking, especially if the lecture is combined with questions that evoke critique and evidence for positions. Beyond its primary uses, lecture is also "efficient," as lots of "content" can be "covered" in a short period of time. A final reason for lecturing is that it provides a common frame of reference to all students, from which discussion and follow-up projects can be launched.

- *Reasons to avoid lecturing.* Lectures can be "deadly." Students report that lectures are "boring." While it is not an ultimate educational goal to entertain, dull presentation of otherwise powerful ideas can smother the fire of interest in students. Lecture provides little opportunity for high affect, except on the part of the lecturer, who is usually having the most interesting time. But lectures do not have to be so desultory. They often fail because they are poorly organized, indifferently delivered, and seemingly irrelevant to students' interests. All lectures inevitably suffer from lack of direct connection to experience; therefore students may not find it easy to transfer lecture-based learning to the field of practice. There are ways to at least minimize the negative aspects of lecture.

If, after weighing these factors, you choose to lecture, or even present a "mini-lecture," then note the following guidelines that Freiberg and Driscoll (1996) suggest, ones that seem to keep lectures vibrant and help students make better sense of the material.

- *Prepare well.* Know the material. Read the original material, then find and/or review supplemental information, recite and jot down or highlight key ideas. Find interesting background information on issues, such as the origins of a theory and the gender and other cultural issues related to the theory.

- *Provide a logical and hierarchical organization of concepts.* Present major points, and then evidence supporting them. Do not flit. Do not digress. Do not report disconnected facts.

- *Begin with an overview of the topic and the learning goals.* Include why you believe that lecture is important at this point.

- *Connect the content.* Relate content to previous and subsequent topics and classes and to applications that the students might engage in—projects, papers, field experiences.

- *Use examples.* Avoid too much abstraction. Ground concepts in concrete illustrations. "Over-abstraction" is a major flaw of lecturing and a reason for poor retention, understanding, and application.

- *Exhibit enthusiasm.* Don't lead in with world-weariness or your own boredom with the topic. Know the material. Enthusiasm and spontaneity arise from the bed of solid preparation. Acknowledge areas in which you lack knowledge, but try not to have many.

- *Keep a pace.* Match the students' understanding—there is a danger of going too fast when *you* know the topic well. Don't over-stimulate. On the other hand, don't go too slowly. Check in regularly with students about their level of understanding and if they have any questions or comments.

- *Vary the presentation.* Use humor, pausing at key points, punctuating at an especially important concept with voice tone or gestures, and physically moving to a different space to introduce another or an important topic. Begin with an anecdote. Pause after a while for a few minutes to let pairs of students share notes and comments on what they understand up to that point.

- *Use visual and auditory media.* Access at least one sense besides hearing. Students report that they greatly appreciate overheads (especially computerized ones) and handouts.

- *Combine lecture with other methods.* Include demonstration, role-play, and discussion. Make the discussion a "critical" one by asking what might be another perspective on this concept. Ask students to give evidence for their ideas.

Perhaps I can illustrate how these ten points might be integrated into a lecture on Holland's theory of matching personality and environment. Many adult education principles are embedded in this illustration, such as personalizing, using experience, being concrete, stimulating reflection, requiring critique, incorperating emotional and motivation, starting simply, and instigating activity.

In this lecture I might begin by asking the students to write down a job or activity that they had disliked and the reasons for their displeasure. I would post these reasons on the board. I then could share an analogy about colors or shapes or and matching—being a "blue" person in a "red" environment, or a "square peg" trying to fit into a "round hole." After this concrete and personalized simple beginning, I segue into the lecture by reminding them that "matching" is a central notion in Holland's theory. I would bring in the "affective" or motivational piece by pointing out their distress in athisdisliked job and its connection to the mismatch with their interests and abilities. I then would offer an overview and outline of the presentation, starting with simple notions such as Holland's basic postulates and ending up with the complexities of congruence and differentiation in the hexagon. I would also at some point share the origins of the theory in prior personality theory, so students might "deconstruct" it.

I would illustrate the six Holland types by noting the probable Holland codes of famous people or characters from popular media characters from film. I would share my enthusiasm for the explanatory power of the model (or the danger of it, if I saw it that way). I would illustrate further by telling of my own job dissatisfactions that were due to the mismatching of my personality (SAI) and the work environment, or my discomfort in auto repair garages, or my bungled attempts and distaste for "Realistic" and "Conventional" activities, such as, house repair and financial record-keeping. I would then ask them to work in groups to discuss their own results on the previously taken Self-Directed Search and to "play" with implied occupations in the Occupations Finder. Thus they would engage in "active experimentation" (Kolb, 1984) in a number of ways. I would have students integrate Holland's model to their later projects, which might consist of doing a "career self-assessment" and an informational interview with a worker.

I would extend the textbook material by showing them how the Holland codes can be used to assess career dissatisfaction. And I would ask them to think critically about the limits of the Self-Directed Search, which may underestimate some individuals' potentials, especially regarding gender and class, because past experience partially predicts test results. Then we would return at the next session for a critique of the theory and its uses.

Perhaps I would have stimulated some critical thinking by such a lecture. Now the students would at least share a common foundation for further discussion and excursions into application. I have no guarantee that they will have heard what I said, however. I would need to assess their understanding by direct inquiry, which might consist of their writing the main points down, as they conceive them, at the end of the session or e-mailing me responses to several questions about the lecture.

QUESTIONING

Questions cant be used to invite critical thinking about issues in a lecture. More broadly, questions can be an invitation for students to become authors of their own ideas, that is, through selective questioning, learners can be invited to contribute their perspectives to the received knowledge. The contribution of questions depends on how they are used—merely to invite fact repetition or, in contrast, to probe multiple views on an open issue. Bothoth can be valuable, but they are vastly different.

Socrates used questions as a means to probe and reason. Similarly, during the Enlightenment questions were seen as superior to reliance on authority and to be an entry into the power of human reason. Both affirmed human construction, rather than some "found" version, of knowledge. As such, questions can move students away from authority-centered knowing to more autonomous construction of ideas.

Asking questions does not guarantee deep reasoning. Kerry (1987) found that the overwhelming majority (96.4%) of questions asked by faculty are requests for facts, and not for application, synthesis, or evaluation, to use Bloom's now famous ascending taxonomy (Bloom, 1956). Socrates would have it otherwise.

But we must be fore warned: If we ask questions, we may get responses! And that is daunting to many instructors. We might not want to know how well students understand, especially if we ourselves are "thin" in our understanding of the subject at hand. We might lose control of time and content if we invite student responses, especially when we probe for reasons, examples, and counter-arguments from students. We must know our content quite deeply to probe at such a level. But such risks are inherent in the constructivist endeavor, so let us step willingly into the unknown territory of inquiry.

The Purposes of Questions

Checking for understanding. In addition to the primary purpose of increasing students' complexity and self-authorship of ideas, questions also serve as a check on student understanding and on instructional effectiveness. The most common model for classroom questioning is when the instructor gives information and asks for recall of facts. That pattern serves the purpose of checking for minimal understanding. It is useful in the context of "facts and skills instruction." We might use it when probing student memory of such counseling content as the origins of the counseling field, the characteristics of Gestalt therapy, the stages of racial identity, or the sequence to be used in reflecting feelings.

"Deepening" thinking. A second major value of using questions in teaching is quite different: It is to deepen student thinking. Students who can give reasons for ideas will become more self-sufficient as professsionals because they can make choices based on evidence. Here is a reminder of Bloom's taxonomy:

- *Application.* Students can mentally apply an idea in practice, living out the abstractions, at least in imagination.

- *Analysis.* Students can analyze an idea, such as the nature of an ethical code, then can generalize it to multiple contexts, as it becomes an overarching set of principles rather than mere concrete rules.

- *Synthesis.* Students can synthesize seemingly different ideas moving toward the "technical eclecticism" (Lazarus & Beutler, 1993) that characterizes the flexible counselor.

- *Evaluation.* Finally, student-counselors can evaluate ideas with evidence. Thus they can become the probing, skeptical professional who is wary of fads and "true-beliefs."

Let us therefore vow to vary our questions, knowing when we want fact recall and when we want students to claim their birthright as knowledge constructors.

Choices in Asking Questions

We face the following choices when we teach using questions: How? Whom? When? Why? We have addressed the latter under "purposes." We now enter the combined realm of "How?" "Whom?" and "When?" Below are some tips that are derived from Freiberg and Driscoll's (1996) review of teaching literature: (a) preparing and asking the questions themselves, (b) what to do immediately after the question, and (c) what to do after the student responds.

- *Before the asking.* Write questions down. You won't always think of them spontaneously, especially higher-order questions.

- *During the asking.* Ask students to explain how they arrived at answers ("Why do you think that?").

  –Have students write their responses to questions for a few seconds before responding—their strategy assures that all students, especially the more introverted, will generate some thoughts.

  –Watch for the "80-20 factor"—80% of the questions are answered by 20% of the students. Try asking each student in the class, in turn, to tell you one idea learned from the text, last class, or today's class. Allow students to pass if their response has already been given. This "Go Around" increases alertness with less pressure than is true for more pointed types of questioning.

  –To evaluate the effectiveness of their understanding. Do not rely solely on asking the question: "Does everyone understand?" and then relying on the responses of a few students. Many students will be reluctant to admit that they do not understand.

  –Watch your voice tone. For example, an instructor might be rellaying sarcasm and frustration in her or his voice in the case of, "How did you decide that?" or she or he might simply be requesting evidence.

- *Immediately after the asking.* "Wait Time" can be as important as the question itself. Rowe (1976) found that longer wait times resulted in ten significant effects, including increased student confidence in responding, increased length of student responses, more evidence offered in student responses, and increased participation by reportedly less "able" students. The typical pause of only one second after a question often results in increased passivity in students and decreased confidence in their intellectual abilities.

  –In the case of "deep reasoning" questions, (application, analysis, synthesis, and evaluation). The questioner needs to wait three to five seconds after asking.

- *After the student responds.* One option is to acknowledge ("Thank you.") and/or paraphrase the student's response ("So, you're saying that cognitive behavioral counseling may not get to a person's core issues ....").

  –A second option is to extend the notion or to probe further. Ask the student to elaborate, expand, or give an example ("Can you think of a situation in which you would notify a parent about a child?"). Or ask a higher level question: "Yes, we have heard that family loyalty is central to Chinese culture. But suppose the client is trying to break away from family rules. How might you respond? Why?" or "So empathy is said to usually be helpful. Can you think of an instance when it might not be?"

–A third option lies in asking a related question of another student ("Can anyone add another or a contrary example?").

Student Questions

Invite students to ask probing questions, as problem-finding, in comparison with problem-solving only, has been associated with high levels of cognitive complexity, especially with "post-formal reasoning" (Yan & Arlin, 1995). The potential "constructivist counselor" (McAuliffe & Lovell, 1996) would be one who sees the dialectical element in human affairs. She or he would probe the conventional way of counseling, considering their usefulness and their limits, and regularly "reinventing the work."

However, it is "counter-cultural" to encourage such student questions. Mars (1984) found only 60 questions being asked by students across 30 class sessions, 28 of which were fact-oriented or logistical. Only two were "deep." Perhaps we discourage student questioning because we fear that we won't be able to answer. I propose that we instead take a deep breath and welcome student inquiry, even demurral. At the very least, we ought not "punish" questions with clipped responses or defensive annoyance. Instead, we might create opportunities for students to formulate questions. For instance, we might direct them to, "Write down three questions that you have about gay and lesbian issues that haven't been addressed," or "Name your concerns about the limitations of person-centered counseling. In what cases might it be most useful?"

The Limits of Questions

For all of their potential to increase student involvement, questions remain a teacher-centered classroom activity. They in fact inhibit discussion when used exclusively. They also fail educationally when only a few students respond, leaving the rest to drift away or feel inadequate. Additionally, questions can lead to a false sense of security, with the instructor being confident that all students understand, when only a few students have demonstrated understanding or when there is silence at the common lecturer inquiry of "Any questions?" Finally, questions fail to move students toward "self-authorized knowing" when they are of the low-level, recall type.

An opposite problem is also important. A warning is in order, even when questioning is challenging and inclusive, more "dualistic" (Perry, 1970) or "received" knowers (Belenky, Clinchy, Goldberger, & Tarule, 1986) will be frustrated by questions that call for divergent responses. Those students will expect "the answer" to be delivered eventually. Honor their dilemma by sharing your view of the place of "facts" and the importance of pondering temporary, contextually based solutions to problems.

CLASSROOM DISCUSSION

As a former literature major, I am used to discussion. It is a central act in probing a literary text. There is no assumed "truth" in literature, only constant, evidence-based critique. Perhaps literature is always obviously interpretable, part of a socially constructed discourse. At least that has been my experience and it is the stance of the so-called post-modern literary theorists (Eagleton, 1983). The social sciences have gone down a different, positivist path. The student who has studied psychology, political science, economics, statistics, and sociology will mostly remember faculty lectures and the absence of class participation in knowledge-creation.

Counselor education lies in a netherworld between such poles. It has a body of techniques and protocols to be learned, yet the counseling interview and relationship can be viewed as a socially constructed event, as Peterson (2000) has so eloquently reminded us. I suggest that we move back and forth between these two poles of directness and participation, honoring both, depending on the moment and topic. It is, however, the pole of social construction that we more often avoid, despite the strong preference that some of our students seem to have for its favoring of induction, dialogue, activity, and experience (McAuliffe, 2000).

Discussion is one way to express social construction in action. Discussion occurs when students share words with each other and when students and teacher exchange ideas. It is the former circumstance that we will especially promote in this segment, as student-to-student discourse honors the participants as knowledge creators. It is in peer exchange that students can deconstruct the authorities to whose coattails they cling. In this way and in the best of circumstances, the instructor is divested of final knowledge. Through discussion, students can experience the power of their own formulating, called "procedural knowing" (Belenky, et al. 1986).

Instructor Role and Conditions for Discussion

Spontaneous exchange in the classroom is to be valued. It is often timely and riveting. However, in most cases good discussion depends on planning by the instructor, proving the cliche: "The best way to be spontaneous is to be prepared." Such preparation might include instructors assigning students to read about the topic, view something about it, or have another experience related to the topic. Before the class session, instructors can formulate and plan a main question, preferably one that is perplexing, one that invites divergence rather than easy convergence, one that requires students to consider contexts rather than absolutes. Such a main question might include: "How can the school counselor be a helper while also being a social advocate and systems-intervener? Here is a situation. Let's discuss these multiple roles."

In constructivist discussion, students become valuable authors of the emergent ideas. Thus, after the initial instigation, the instructor waits, as described above. A student responds verbally, either voluntarily or by being asked directly. Then the instructor signals non-verbally that she or he has heard and waits again. She or he does not comment on the student's response. Freiberg and Driscoll (1996) warn us: "Because most teachers see their role as being the gatekeeper during questioning, it is difficult to change roles for discussion. *The discussion may become too teacher dominated, which, in fact, foils discussion . . . .*[Italics mine]" (p. 223). Do not take turns with the students. Instead, be a moderator. Move from the role of "giver of information" to "facilitator of information exchange or idea exchange." Most of us have seen few models of the latter in our own schooling. Counselor educators here have an advantage, however, as they have experienced group facilitation themselves.

Here is an example from an actual class of stunted teacher-student discussion:

S1: "If I were a business owner, I wouldn't hire a disabled person if it required the expense of putting in a ramp."

T: "So you really think that the disabled person would have to limit her jobs to accessible facilities and that's ok . . . "

S1: "I guess so . . . ."

Here is an example of student-to-student exchange:

S1: "If I were a business owner, I wouldn't hire a disabled person if it required the expense of putting in a ramp."

S2: "But that would be discriminatory and immoral. It's all of our responsibility to try to create a level playing field . . . ."

S1: "That's not the business owner's job. She has to make a living."

S2: "That isn't always at stake, though."

S3: "I guess it depends on whether it costs too much."
S1: "Maybe large businesses can do it, but small ones can't always."

S2: "That doesn't get rid of the moral question. Get a loan. Find a way to make it profitable—rent it to kids as a skateboard ramp after hours!"

(Laughter from class)

S1: "That's unrealistic, but maybe the disabled employee could help the owner to find an agency that would help with the cost . . . ."

(The students go on parrying about the dual issues of moral responsibility and business profit.)

Instead of jumping in and delivering a summary of the issues, the instructor here let students struggle, nodding occasionally, pointing to students who had their hands up. Most of the students were attentive. The speakers were especially engaged. They had to struggle with a fuzzy situation. They gained confidence. They might now be better able to weigh evidence in future professional problem-solving situations.

As Dewey (Fishman and McCarthy, 1998) has reminded us, it is the means that is the end, the process that is the content. The learning goals of creating critical and dialogical thinkers can be achieved through the process of discussion. In contrast, if the instructor regularly "deposited" the content and gave solutions to dilemmas, students would be left disempowered, dependent on the experts. They would have had little experience with the hard work of dialogue, that is, of formulating questions, listening, tendering tentative solutions, and modifying their ideas based upon hearing those of others. In this sense, discussion can be the entry gate on the royal road to learning the power of dialogue (Yankelovich, 1999).

Students' Roles in Discussion

Obviously, students must be willing to participate in discussion. And, if they are so willing, further conditions must be met for inclusive discussion to take place. The "talkers" will have to moderate their "air time." The less-verbal students will have to proffer their ruminations. In the latter vein, the instructor can encourage all contributions and even require some, as in the above mentioned "Go Around" activity.

Some guidelines can be implemented. Students might be asked to take a minute to write their ideas before the discussion. During the exchange, all will have to agree to not put down others' ideas or personhood—no character assassination or name-calling. Participants will need to actively listen, not shuffle papers or cross-talk. Anyone who speaks should be grounding his or her thinking in the preparatory reading assignment. Instructors can name ground rules early in a semester and ask students for additional guidelines during the semester. Such attention to process models an important skill for future counselors.

And thus this discussion road that leads to procedural knowing winds through many stops, starts, interchanges, and, occasionally, detours. It cannot be straight if it is to be used by all travelers.

CONCLUSION

Here we have acknowledged the pervasiveness of the traditional teaching methods of lecture, questioning, and discussion-leading. However, we have distinguished a flat, passivity-inducing traditional method from one that engages students to be knowledge-constructors themselves.

REFERENCES

Belenky, M., Clinchy, B., Goldberger, N., & Tarule, J. (1986). *Women's ways of knowing*. New York: Basic Books.

Bloom, B. S. (1956). *A taxonomy of educational objectives*. New York: Longman.

Eagleton, T. (1983). *Literary theory: An introduction*. Minneapolis: University of Minnesota Press.

Fishman, S. M., & McCarthy, L. (1998). *John Dewey and the challenge of classroom practice*. New York: Teachers College Press.

Freiberg, H. J., & Driscoll, A. (1996). *Universal teaching strategies*. Boston: Allyn & Bacon.

Kerry, T. (1987). Classroom questions in England. *Questioning Exchange, 1*, 33.

Kolb, D. (1984). *Experiential learning: Experience as the source of learning and development*. Englewood Cliffs, NJ: Prentice Hall.

Lazarus, A., & Beutler, L. E. (1993). On technical eclecticism. *Journal of Counseling and Development, 71*, 381-385.

Mars, J. (1984). Questioning in Czechoslovakia. *Questioning Exchange, 5*, 8-11.

McAuliffe, G. J. (2000). How counselor education influences future helpers: What students say. In G. McAuliffe, K. Eriksen, & Associates (2000). *Preparing counselors and therapists: Creating constructivist and developmental programs*. Alexandria, VA: Association for Counselor Education and Supervision.

McAuliffe, G. J., & Lovell, C. W. (1996). *The making of the constructivist counselor*. Paper presented at the meeting of the Association for Counselor Education and Supervision. Portland, OR.

Perry, W. G. (1970). *Forms of intellectual and ethical development in the college years*. New York: Holt, Rinehart, & Winston.

Peterson, J. S. (2000). Constructing the course of human development. In G. McAuliffe, K. Eriksen, & Associates (2000). *Preparing counselors and therapists: Creating constructivist and developmental programs*. Alexandria, VA: Association for Counselor Education and Supervision, 170-194.

Rowe, M. B. (1976). The pausing principle: Two invitations to inquiry. *Journal of College Science Teaching, 5*, 258-260.

Yan, B., & Arlin, P. K. (1995). Nonabsolute/relativistic thinking: A common factor underlying models of postformal reasoning? *Journal of Adult Development, 2*, 223-240.

Yankelovich, D. (1999). *The magic of dialogue: Transforming conflict into cooperation*. New York: Simon and Schuster.

3

Activities for Increasing Personal Awareness

Karen Eriksen, Nathalie Kees, Rolla E. Lewis,

James McGraw, Carlotta J. Willis, Lois Benishek

"Awareness" has been a watchword for the counseling field, at least since the early days of humanistic psychology. In social constructionist parlance, such awareness is often called "reflexivity." Whatever the language used, the concept represents being vigilant about one's own psychological states, epistemological assumptions, "hidden agendas," cultural biases, and the like. In the following segments, such reflexivity is promoted through both the verbal and non-verbal means of visualization, narrative writing, introspection, film review, group discussion, and observation of one's own reactions. Each exercise is personalized and emotionally evocative. Each challenges future counselors to know the tacit, often pre-verbal dimensions of their "psycho-logic." The hope of such exercises is that students' future work might be freer of projection and prejudice, and more humble and tuned to the social construction of the counseling process.

—Garrett McAuliffe

THE FEELINGS ROUND
—Karen Eriksen

In the 1970's, "How are you feeling?" became known as such a standard therapist question that even commonly sold "therapist" dolls parroted that phrase to make people laugh. And yet, it seems that despite the focus on feelings during that era of the so called "me" generation, our society—and thus our students—have not become any better at identifying and express-

ing feelings. Feeling awareness and conscience are not passed on geneti-
cally; each generation must learn themanew. And thus, counselors often
find themselves checking in with people about how they feel or teaching
them how to name their feelings. And counselor educators feel that they need
to teach their students about feelings so that those counselors-to-be might be
able to work on a feeling level with their future clients or students. The "Feelings Round" exercise assists students to discuss and describe feelings at differing levels of vulnerability, serves as a model for students' future efforts at
trying to get their clients to do the same, and launches discussions about the
use of feelings and reflections of feelings in counseling sessions.

Bill Bruck, formerly of Marymount University, developed the Feelings
Round as an exercise for the Group Counseling course (personal communication, 1995. First, he developed a "taxonomy" of feelings (see Appendix), in which he categorized feeling words by type. Next, in feeling
"rounds," he asked students to use the taxonomy to identify and describe
their own feelings, beginning with the more ambiguous and safe feelings
and progressively moving toward more precise and descriptive feeling labels, ones whose expression increased student vulnerability.

Benefits of the Feelings Round Activity

Learning about feelings. The Feelings Round exercise offers an inductive
and active method for teaching about the nature of feelings and feeling
expression. Students gain an understanding of what qualifies as a feeling,
of the range of feelings that might be experienced and expressed, and of
what feelings might be more or less difficult to express. They discover that
those feelings that are harder to express are often more useful to the counseling process and contribute to a greater understanding of the client.

Students also gain an understanding of the complexity of people's feeling lives. That is, they hear their peers—who share their own student status and experiences—and express a wide range of different feelings. They
hear these other students owning several different feelings at the same
moment in class. They discover that when someone indicates that he or
she feels "bad," it does not mean that the person does not have some good
feelings as well. They discover that the first words out of a person's mouth
rarely capture the person's full experience. Hearing the multiple perspectives of other students consequently deepens their own understandings of
feelings and feeling expression.

Further, students personally discover how difficult it is to identify and express feelings. Discussions following such discoveries allow students to hear
to consider what their future clients' or students' reportygovs are likely to be
when asked about their feelings.

Incorporating adult learning principles. The Feelings Round exercise is grounded in adult learning principles, in that the experience engages students actively, grounds professional learning in the personal, and emphasizes the benefits of learning in community. For instance, students actively risk describing their own feelings, listen to others expressing feelings, engage in meta-communication about the experience of identifying and describing feelings, and explore the importance of understanding feelings and feeling expression to their future as counselors. They thus actively "co-construct" with their peers and instructor their understandings about the nature and importance about feelings.

Students also translate learning from the personal to the professional context and back again. They begin with the personal, that is, identifying and discussing the feelings they are currently experiencing. They then consider the relevance to their professional life of knowing about feelings. They can later use such lessons about emotions in their personal lives. For instance, some students who carefully search the Feelings List for a feeling word to describe what they are experiencing at the moment, may find themselves to be surprised at the number of feelings that exist. They may in turn discover how difficult it is to find a word or two to fully describe their own current experience. After students explore the importance of feeling awareness to the counseling endeavor, they find themselves more committed to remaining aware of their own feeling lives. After all, how can they expect clients and students to delve into deeper feeling levels if they are unwilling to do so themselves? Thus students take the "personal" back into their professional lives by attending more fully to their own and others' feelings and feeling descriptions and by expanding the numbers of feelings they bring to awareness.

Such connections between the personal and the professional are further illustrated by the instructor's sharing of his or her own feelings (that is bringing personal feelings into the professional arena). Students thus see modeled a unity or strong connection between the counselor's professional and personal life.

An additional benefit lies in the creation of a class community. Because expressing feelings is a personal and vulnerable process, and because of the active, egalitarian co-construction of knowledge involved in this exercise, students find themselves feeling more connected with each other in a caring community. Such a community offers people the safety and freedom to explore their own and others' perspectives and allows for creative and free-flowing dialogue, both of which are helpful to future learning. A connected community of learners might be particularly necessary for counseling courses because of the personal material that is shared as a matter of course.

Finally, learning on multiple levels—for example, simultaneously at the cognitive and the affective levels—promotes future retention and application to practice.

Promoting student development. The Feelings Round exercise promotes student development. Discovering the range of feelings that might exist challenges students to attend to and become aware of a wider range of feelings within themselves, which may deepen their emotional lives. The Feelings Round also challenges students to consider multiple perspectives (such as differing feelings held, often at the same time, by their peers, or feelings that are triggered by a variety of life situations), and to voice their own perspectives. These enhance cognitive development (Kegan, 1982, 1994). The "challenge" of trusting more internal ways of knowing rather than only trusting knowledge that comes from external authorities is necessary for movement from a convention-reliant way of knowing to a "self-authoring" (Kegan, 1982, 1994), "conscientious" (Loevinger, 1976), or "procedural" way of knowing (Belenky, Clinchy, Goldberger, & Tarule, 1986).

Further, co-construction of knowledge is also a developmental achievement, and, when introduced with support, can thus challenge students to progress developmentally. Such a challenge may occur, for instance, as the instructor poses questions about possibilities (such as, types of feelings, why feelings are difficult to express, the benefits to counseling of knowing about feelings). Posing questions may encourage student dialogue on feelings and feeling expression, and typically instigates students to engage in mutually constructing new possibilities. The instructor can then punctuate such possibilities by adding his or her own perspectives and experiences to student ideas. The Feelings Round can mentally bring students into class.

Opening the class. After an initial introduction of the exercise, the instructor may choose to use an abbreviated version to begin a class session. When used thus, the exercise moves students fully into the classroom from wherever else they have been psychically: at work, driving the highway, thinking about their kids, having an argument with a friend. For adult students who find themselves stretched between work, family, and school, such focusing at the beginning of class can be quite important.

An "advance organizer." A final benefit of the exercise is that it "warns" students about what is to come during the rest of the class, and perhaps during the rest of their graduate program. That is, students become aware that this course, and counselor education in general, involves the personal, requires them to grow, and challenges them to search themselves. As an advance organizer, the exercise also serves as a natural entré into further discussions about the micro skill of "reflection of feelings," and about taking counseling sessions to a deeper level. While such discussions may begin in the Counseling Skills course, they may also emerge in any skills-focused course, such as Group Counseling, Practicum, or Internship.

Objectives

Increase future counselors:

- attention to clients' and students' feelings, and the levels of vulnerability expressed by different feelings

- knowledge of the range of feelings and of a useful taxonomy for classifying them

- understanding of the usefulness to the counseling process of helping a client or student to express feelings

- awareness of their own feeling states

Description of the Activity

The activity proceeds through seven "rounds," followed by a discussion of the experience. Initially, the instructor asks students to go around the room one by one—with permission to pass if they must—saying one word that captures how they are presently feeling. Students typically express feelings ranging from "sad" to "overwhelmed" to "frazzled" to "tired" (In the Counseling Skills course, it might be noted, this exercise usually occurs fairly close to the third or fourth week of the semester). The instructor then asks, "Which feelings that were expressed seemed harder to say?" and "Which feelings allowed you to know the person more fully?" During the discussion on these questions, students begin to classify feelings into those that are about a person's emotions, or those that are about a person's physical state. There is a difference in depth and risk: Students note that those feelings that are harder to say and allow the group to know a person more fully usually seem to also leave the speaker more vulnerable.

Once students have begun to identify some qualitative differences among feelings, the instructor structures the subsequent rounds so that the feelings progress from safer and more vague to more vulnerable and descriptive. For instance, during round two, the instructor asks students to express only whether they generally feel "bad" or "good." The instructor then hands out the taxonomy of feelings, and in round three, asks students to express feelings related to their physical state. Next follow rounds on feelings about "attention" or "cognition," feelings related to "will," and feelings that are positively or negatively emotional. Finally, the instructor asks students to go around and say one or two sentences, if they wish, about why they might be feeling any particular feeling.

During class discussion following the activity, the instructor asks students questions such as the following: "What did you notice in the classroom as you did this?" "What did you notice in yourself?" "Are there any feelings you just don't 'do?'" "Are there those that are more difficult for you to express?" "What relevance do you think this activity has for work with clients or students?" "Why do we care about clients' or students' feelings?" "When might we refrain from exploring feelings?" Students have many interesting responses to such questions. As mentioned above in the introduction, students generally notice a change in the atmosphere of the room to one that seems more intimate and caring. They also talk about the difficulties they had expressing some feelings, and about difficulties in figuring out exactly what they felt. Often they report that they had no idea that there were so many feelings, even though clearly any list provided would necessarily be incomplete.

Students are also often amazed and surprised at the complexity of emotional life. Thus the idea of "mixed feelings" can be highlighted. For instance, questions emerge about how someone who says she feels good can also feel nervous, or how can someone who says he feels "bad" also say he feels excited about what is happening in class? How is it possible for one person to experience several feelings at one time? Students' translation of this awareness to their future as counselors seems almost automatic and immediate. Very little prompting is necessary in their discussions about how they will use this experience and information in their future work.

In general, I close the discussion with a caution about the risks of and conditions for delving into deeper feeling levels with clients, and of when I choose not to explore feelings with clients. For instance, more disturbed clients who are out of control behaviorally or emotionally may need a counselor who helps them to contain their emotions, rather than urging them to express them. But even "normal" clients—and some of our students—who have never considered operating on a feeling level may begin to discover a new way of communicating, being intimate, and experiencing the world. Such a discovery may significantly change their relationships and what they want out of life. Clearly any such change brings with it uncertainties and risks. While we may believe that such change is good, some people may not be ready for it, and significant others in these people's lives may find the changes threatening and unwanted.

CONCLUSION

The "feelings round" activity offers students an introduction to the world of feelings, to their own and their clients' feelings, and to the place of "feeling description" in the counseling process. It offers students an opportunity for inductive learning. It fosters student self-discovery and cognitive development.

APPENDIX
Feelings List

Physical State
Unhealthy
    Weak
    Feverish
    [Sick]
    Achy
    In pain

Tired
    Sleepy
    Drowsy
    Drained
    Exhausted
    Fatigued
    Weary

Energized
    Awake
    Charged
    Excited

"Nervous energy"
    Excited
    Stirred up
    Edgy
    Fidgety
    Jumpy
    Agitated

Physically relaxed
    Refreshed
    Relaxed
    Rested

Physically tense
    Tense
    Tight

Attention or Cognition
Being intellectually drawn
    Fascinated
    Curious
    Interested
    Intrigued
    Stimulated
    Motivated

Being surprised
    Surprised
    Astonished
    Astounded
    Stunned

Being not engaged
    Apathetic
    Bored
    Detached
    Indifferent
    Lackadaisical
    Uninterested

Being confused
    Confused
    Flustered
    Baffled
    Bewildered
    Perplexed
    Puzzled

Being unable to concen-trate
    Distracted
    Preoccupied

"Will"
Feelings related to power
    Empowered
    Powerful
    Forceful
    Strong
    Competent

Feelings related to powerlessness
    Weak
    Powerless
    Incompetent
    Submissive

Feelings related to not wanting to do something
    Unwilling
    Reluctant
    Disinclined

Being ambivalent or unsure
    Hesitant
    Ambivalent
    Unsure
    Dubious
    Indecisive
    Tentative

Feelings related to persistence
    Stubborn
    Adamant
    Determined
    Obstinate
    Self-righteous
    Tenacious

Feelings like "doing the opposite of"
    Rebellious
    Contrary
    Defiant

Positive Emotional
Responses to good things that have happened
    Grateful
    Gratified
    Fortunate
    Relieved
    Satisfied
    Thankful

Feelings of good fellowship
    Congenial
    Agreeable
    Affable
    Cordial

Generally happy feelings
    Happy
    Cheerful
    Delighted

(Continued)

Feelings List *(continued)*

Positive feelings towards others
- Admiration
- Respectful
- Trusting
- Attracted

Extremely happy feelings
- Ecstatic
- Overjoyed
- Elated
- Exuberant
- Euphoric
- Jubilant

Responses to others care/attention
- Relieved
- Comforted
- Consoled
- Exonerated
- Soothed

Humorous or lighthearted feelings
- Amused
- Jovial
- Merry
- Lighthearted
- Silly

Passively positive
- Complacent
- Content
- Sanguine
- Satisfied

Response to anticipated good things to come
- Optimistic
- Confident
- Enthusiastic

Negative Emotional
Distrustful or shy feelings
- Deceived
- Diffident
- Dislike
- Distrust

- Shy
- Suspicion
- Timid

Feelings about "bad" things we've done
- Guilty
- Humiliated
- Dismayed
- Ashamed
- Embarrassed

Anxious or worried type feelings
- Afraid
- Anxious
- Apprehensive
- Concerned
- Distressed
- Frightened
- Panicky
- Scared
- Terrified
- Uneasy
- Unsettled
- Worried

Resentful
- Envious
- Jealous
- Possessive

Lonely type feelings
- Lonely
- Alone
- Forlorn
- Isolated
- Lonesome
- Rejected

Depressed
- Blue
- Depressed
- Despair
- Discouraged
- Down
- Melancholy

Angry type feelings
- Angry
- Aggravated
- Annoyed
- Antagonistic
- Belligerent
- Bitter
- Cross
- Cranky
- Disgusted
- Embittered
- Enraged
- Exasperated
- Furious
- Hostile
- Incensed
- Indignant
- Irate
- Irritated
- Mad
- Outraged
- Vengeful
- Wrathful

Sad
- Dejected
- Desolate
- Despairing
- Disappointed
- Distressed
- Forlorn
- Gloomy
- Grieving
- Heartbroken
- Inconsolable
- Melancholy

Frustrated
- Circumvented
- Confounded
- Hindered
- Thwarted

REFERENCES

Belenky, M., Clinchy, B., Goldberger, N., & Tarule, J. (1986). *Women's ways of knowing*. New York: Basic Books.

Kegan, R. (1982). *The evolving self*. Cambridge, MA: Harvard University Press.

Kegan, R. (1994). *In over our heads: The mental demands of modern life*. Cambridge: Harvard University Press.

Loevinger, J. (1976). *Ego development: Conceptions and theories*. San Francisco: Jossey-Bass.

GUIDED VISUALIZATION
—Nathalie Kees

Beginning counselors often experience a developmental crisis in their skill acquisition that I refer to as "hitting the wall." Midway through their skill development, many students say, "I was a better counselor before I entered the program," or "All of these theories and skills are getting in the way." They lament the seeming loss of their natural abilities as listeners and helpers and experience the anxiety and integration difficulties common to any new skill acquisition. The purpose here is to share two guided visualizations that I use with beginning counseling students in order to create a safe and student-centered learning environment, reduce anxiety, and help students "get over the wall".

Guided visualization has been used as an aid to skill acquisition and anxiety reduction in several fields, including nursing and health care education (Cassel, 1991; Contrades, 1991; Speck, 1990; Tynn, 1994), engineering education (Braukmann & Pedras, 1993), physics education (Nakaii, 1991), and drama, theatre, and speech education (Ayres, 1995; Norris, 1995). The terms guided visualization and guided imagery are used interchangeably in the literature. They refer to internally visualizing an action or situation in order to (a) improve performance of a skill through visual practice or (b) reduce anxiety through concurrent visualization and relaxation (Gawain, 1982).

From a constructivist standpoint, visualization helps students clarify their individual contexts and "pre-understandings" prior to adding new subject matter (McAuliffe & Lovell, 2000) and allows the instructor to build skill acquisition and course content on students' pre-existing knowledge and experiences. Meaningful connections between the subject matter and students' foundational understandings may be made, paving the way for creating learning environments in which traditional distinctions among teacher, learner, and course content begin to dissolve (Palmer, 1993; 1998).

Instructor and students experience many benefits from guided visualization. Students' already existing inner resources become accessible. Learner readiness for acquiring new skills and information can be assessed. Additionally, students experience a present-centeredness and focus that they find helpful in taping practice sessions or seeing clients. Thus, they ask for taped copies of the inner counselor visualization to use in recreating this focus. Several students have requested, however, that the instructor let them know up front that they will be inviting another person into the space they are visualizing so they may mentally prepare a communal rather than solitary setting. This is particularly important for students whose trust and/or personal spaces have been violated in the past. Some students have been amazed at the clarity of their personal goal-setting visualizations, and at how these images have been manifested by the end of the course. Other students have remarked that visualization has helped them remain focused and personally invested in their learning throughout the semester.

As with other constructivist approaches, the visualizations help establish a classroom environment of shared experience, trust, and mutual respect. The reduction of anxiety removes unnecessary barriers to learning and to performing complex, multidimensional, and multisensory tasks, of which counseling is a prime example.

Objectives

- Inner Counselor Visualization:

  To *reduce* student performance anxiety when demonstrating counseling skills.

  To *improve* student performance of counseling skills through visual preparation and practice.

- Personal Goal-Setting Visualization:

  To *clarify* students' goals for a course.

  To *revise* course content and instructional methods based upon student input and goals.

Description of Activities

Inner counselor visualization. During the first or second session of a basic counseling-skills course, prior to the introduction of content, the instructor guides students through a visualization to access their "inner counselor." The "inner counselor" represents the naturally empathic, present-centered, and competent listener within each of them, which may have served as the original impetus for entering a helping profession.

Students receive an explanation of the purpose and process of the guided visualization and discuss their familiarity and comfort level with these techniques. I provide alternative choices and options for those who might be uncomfortable with visualization. Such options also enhance safety and security for those willing to participate. Options include keeping their eyes open if that increases their sense of safety and comfort, or accessing a higher power if that feels more comfortable than utilizing an internal source.

Once the instructor has established a safe and informed setting, students make themselves comfortable and participate in a short relaxation procedure. Numerous methods for relaxation exist, including alternate muscle tensing and relaxing and/or deep breathing.

After the relaxation procedure, students imagine themselves in a place that feels safe and comfortable. This place may be real or imagined. Once there, they continue breathing and accessing a sense of relaxation and calm. The instructor then invites them to bring into their space a friend or acquaintance with whom they feel comfortable and who wishes to talk to them about concerns, issues, or happenings in their lives. The instructor guides the students to be fully present, as helpful reflections and questions emerge from a place of unconditional regard. When guiding visualizations, it is important for the instructor to include words which access the various learning modalities, that is, visual, kinesthetic, and auditory, of all students (King, Novik, & Citrenbaum, 1983), such as, "Picture yourself . . .", "What are you feeling as you . . .", and "What would you tell yourself about . . .". A sample narration follows.

Imagine yourself in a place in which you feel comfortable and into which you would be willing to invite someone you know. Continue breathing and relaxing as you imagine that person coming in and sitting down. Imagine yourself becoming fully present to this person, giving them your full attention. As the person begins speaking to you, imagine yourself listening intently, feeling what the other is feeling, and seeing the world through their eyes. Absorb what the other is saying . . . what it is like to be in that other person's shoes. You feel completely present-centered and focused on the other person. All other thoughts and distractions vanish. You are able to listen unconditionally to what the other is saying, and from this place of unconditional positive regard, appropriate responses emerge. Remember to breathe and relax as you do so. You are able to reflect back to the person what they are feeling and saying. You are able to reflect not only what is said, also what the other may only be alluding to. From this place of feeling centered, open-ended questions emerge, which help the other person think more deeply about what they are telling you. As you are listening, time seems to fly by. You are completely absorbed in what is happening and an hour seems like minutes. You are aware that you have accessed your inner counselor. It is the part of you that is a natural listener and helper, the part of you that enjoys working with others and helping them clarify their needs and direction, the natural helper within you that has led you to choose a counseling profession.

As their time with the other person comes to a close, the instructor asks students to use a Neuro-Linguistic Programming (NLP) technique called "anchoring" to retain this feeling of being present-centered and completely focused. Various anchoring techniques exist (Andreas & Andreas, 1989; King et al., 1983). One technique that I have used successfully is to have students squeeze both of their hands together, locking in the kinesthetic and emotional memory of the experience and being able to recreate the desired response whenever they again squeeze their hands. Then, counting backward from five to one, the instructor brings students back to the present room and time with suggestions to retain the sense of calm, relaxation, and alertness. Upon completion, the class processes the visualization experience verbally or in writing, responding to questions such as, "What do you want to remember from that experience?" and "How will you apply or use what you have learned?"

Students may repeat this exercise later in the course in order to integrate the abundant content and skills practiced during that semester. They may also repeat it prior to seeing their first clients in order to reduce anxiety and increase present awareness and focus. In this situation, students would visualize listening to someone they don't know while continuing to practice relaxation and breathing techniques.

Personal goal-setting visualization. I have also used guided visualization in other contexts, such as helping students create their personal goals for a course. On the first day of class, the instructor leads students through a visualization in which they imagine themselves leaving class on the last day of the semester. The instructor asks students to reflect on questions such as, "How am I different?", "What do I know, think, feel, or do differently?", and "Where am I going from here?" Students then visualize themselves leaving the building. As they exit through the door, students see their reflection in a window or mirror. The instructor asks students to have a conversation with that image, responding to questions such as, "What do you say to that image of yourself?" and "How does your reflection respond?"

Students then return to the present place and time and discuss what they need from themselves, each other, the course, and the instructor in order to accomplish or enhance their vision. The instructor is able to refine course content and instruction based upon student input. Students write down their personal goals and refer to them throughout the course, assessing their accuracy at the end of the semester.

REFERENCES

Andreas, C. & Andreas, S. (1989). *Heart of the mind*. Moab, UT: Real People Press.

Ayres, J. (1995). A component analysis of performance visualization. *Communication Reports, 8,* 185-92.

Braukmann, J. & Pedras, M. J. (1993). A comparison of two methods of teaching visualization skills to college students. *Journal of Industrial Teacher Education, 30,* 65-72.

Cassel, R. N. (1991). Tracing the evolution of guided imagery theory in relation to health care. *Education, 112,* 300.

Contrades, S. (1991). Guided imagery use in nursing education. *Journal of Holistic Nursing, 9,* 62-68.

Gawain, S. (1982). *Creative visualization*. Toronto: Bantam Books.

King, M., Novik, L., & Citrenbaum, C. (1983). *Irresistible communication: Creative skills for the health professional*. Philadelphia: W. B. Saunders Company.

McAuliffe, G., & Lovell, C. (2000). Encouraging transformation: Guidelines for constructivist and developmental instruction. In G. McAuliffe, K. Eriksen, and Associates, *Preparing counselors and therapists: Creating constructivist and developmental programs* (pp. 14-41). Alexandria, VA: Association for Counselor Education and Supervision.

Nakaii, D. M. (1991). Classroom research in physics: Gaining insights into visualization and problem solving. *New Directions for Teaching and Learning, 46,* 79-87.

Norris, J. (1995). Response-able guided imagery. *Stage of the Art, 7,* 4-9.

Palmer, P. J. (1993). *To know as we are known: Education as a spiritual journey*. San Francisco: Harper.

Palmer, P. J. (1998). *The courage to teach: Exploring the inner landscape of a teacher's life*. San Francisco: Jossey-Bass.

Speck, B. J. (1990). The effect of guided imagery upon first semester nursing students performing their first injections. *The Journal of Nursing Education, 29,* 346-350.

Tynn, L. K. (1994). Using guided imagery exercises in the classroom. *The Journal of Nursing Education, 33,* 157-158.

THE STRUCTURED NARRATIVE EXERCISE
—*Rolla E. Lewis*

Beginning counselors often lose sight of their own competencies. During the Structured Narrative exercise, students combat this problem by examining the notion that clients and professionals "story" their lives and that professional competence is an evolving story (White & Epston, 1990; Epston & White, 1995).

In introducing students to Structured Narrative, I point to the range of work supporting the use of writing in therapy. Riordan (1996) offers a summary of such evidence. Pennebaker and his colleagues (1986, 1988, 1989, 1990, 1994, 1997) have conducted a number of studies showing the value of writing in therapy. L'Abate (1992) offers a programmed approach to using writing in therapy, whereas Sarbin (1986), White and Epston (1990), and Monk, Winslade, Crocket, and Epston (1997) draw upon the narrative tradition in the counseling field. In that tradition, Epston and White (1995) specifically describe a counseling approach called "systemically informed constructivist thinking" that is designed to help clients gain authorship over the story of their lives.

Such authors indicate that the act of writing deepens and clarifies our thoughts and provides us with a "snapshot" of the thoughts and narratives we have in progress. As a technology deeply embedded in culture, writing captures us either in our honesty or in our earnest attempts to manipulate a story in a favored direction. Structured Narrative is a one approach for introducing students to the history of writing in counseling. Structured Narrative also offers a format for orienting students to specific expectations inherent in programs of study, for assessing their current thoughts and perceptions about entering a profession, and for enabling them to reflect on what they have thought or perceived in the past about themselves and their personal competencies. Structured Narrative is designed to help counselor education students make the transition into a new profession and into the counselor education program, a transition that can be stressful because of the many simultaneously occurring changes it involves. Constructivist counselor educators want students to assess, reflect upon, and develop philosophies about becoming counselors. Structured Narrative is a tool for documenting this process.

Structured Narrative specifically helps students to understand the narrative impulse in counseling practice. After reviewing her Structured Narrative lessons, one student commented, "I've moved from being very uncertain and unsure. I think I was problem-oriented. Now, I'm more solution-oriented, constantly looking for ways to make things better. I'm much more confident and capable . . . . I'm not stuck . . . . I no longer feel the need to do it alone." In reviewing Structured Narratives students are able to tap into what Claxton (1997) calls "slower ways of knowing" that emerge indirectly from our intuitions and reflections. They are able to step outside of themselves and see their professional story as evolving constantly.

Structured Narrative benefits students in other ways as well. By focusing on competency, the Structured Narrative activity helps students see themselves and fellow students as having different resources, personally and professionally (for example, sports, cooking, gardening). Large group sharing helps create a sense of a community. End of term follow-up helps students to see how their perspectives are situated in time and context.

Structured Narratives are useful for different courses throughout the counselor preparation program, such as in Foundations of School Counseling, Practicum, Internship, and Guidance for the Classroom Teacher. Topics of narratives may include such subjects as celebrating competence, fostering resiliency, and school-to-work programs. Narrative exercises may be developed to fit the needs of a wide-variety of classes.

Objectives

- Increase students' sense of competence, and their awareness of where that sense comes from.

- Introduce students to the history of writing in counseling.

- Ease students' transition into a new profession and into the counselor education program.

- Assist students to tap into knowing that emerges from intuition and reflection.

Description of Activity

The activity occurs in two or three parts: 1) At the beginning of the term have the students complete the Structured Narrative questionnaire below. 2) Upon completing the assignment, ask the students to share the results of their Structured Narrative with a group of 3-4 fellow students. 3) Toward the end of the term, have the students revisit the assignment's theme to assess if their own "preferred description" is in alignment with their practice as a counselor (White & Epston, 1990). Below is a description of one such narrative.

SAMPLE STRUCTURED NARRATIVE: "VISION OF SELF AS A COUNSELOR"

Describe the Following to the Students:

"Assuming the principle that 'what you see (theorize) is what you get,' the Structured Narrative exercises asks you take a "snapshot" of yourself as a counselor—even if you are not currently a counselor. At several points during the course we will return to your "snapshot" to determine if you envision yourself differently or would like to as a result of what you have learned in the course.

The purpose of this exercise is to explore your perception of yourself as a professional and to develop your story as a person growing toward greater understanding, wisdom, and compassion. If you are uncomfortable with any of the questions, ponder what has been asked but do not feel compelled to write."

Narrative Prompts:

(NOTE: Each prompt is followed by one to twenty blank lines for written responses. The limits set by the pre-printed blank lines require parsimony and define the preferred length for student responses.)

Personal Vision

- Describe any special talents you have (such as, a second or third language, music, art, storytelling, culinary arts).

- In the course of your life, who do you see as your best teacher? Why?

- List four qualities they possessed or lessons they taught you:

- What do you see as your inner resources?

- Look back in time; describe a time when you were not concerned about yourself or the impression you were making on others?

Professional Vision

- Imagine yourself bringing these talents and resources into your new profession. Describe the competencies that you see.

- How would you describe your potential role as a counselor?

- What do you see that you have to learn or do in order to become the counselor that you want to be?

- What picture comes to mind as you imagine yourself doing counseling?

- How do you want your clients to remember you as a counselor?

- How would you like your colleagues to see and describe you as a professional?

- What do you see as your best attribute as a counselor?

REFERENCES

Claxton, G. (1997). *Hare brain, tortoise mind: Why intelligence increases when you think less.* Hopewell, NJ: The Ecco Press.

Epston, D., White, M. (1995). Termination as a rite of passage: Questioning strategies for a therapy of inclusion. In R. A. Neimeyer & M. J. Mahoney (Eds.), *Constructivism in counseling* (pp. 339-354). Washington, DC: American Psychological Association.

L'Abate, L. (1992). *Programmed writing: A paratherapeutic approach for intervention with individuals, couples, and families.* Pacific Grove, CA: Brooks/Cole.

Lewis, R. E. (1999) A write way: Fostering resiliency during transitions. *Humanistic Counseling, Education, and Development, 37,* 200-211.

Monk, G., Winslade, J., Crocket, K., & Epston, D. (Eds.). (1997). *Narrative therapy in practice: The archaeology of hope.* San Francisco: Jossey-Bass Publishers.

Pennebaker, J. W. (1989). Confession, inhibition, and disease. In L. Berkowitz (Ed.), *Advances in experimental social psychology, Vol. 22.* (pp. 211-244). New York: Springer-Verlag.

Pennebaker, J. W. (1990). *Opening up: The healing power of confiding in others.* New York: Avon.

Pennebaker, J. W. (1997). *Opening up: The healing power of expressing emotions.* New York: Guilford.

Pennebaker, J. W., & Beall, S. K. (1986). Confronting a traumatic event: Toward an understanding of inhibition and disease. *Journal of Abnormal Psychology, 95,* 274-281.

Pennebaker, J. W., Kiecolt-Glaser, J. K., & Glaser, R. (1988). Disclosure of traumas and immune function: Health implications for counseling. *Journal of Consulting and Clinical Psychology, 56,* 239-245.

Riordan, R. J. (1996). Scriptotherapy: Therapeutic writing as a counseling adjunct. *Journal of Counseling and Development, 74,* 263-269.

Sarbin , T. R. (Ed.). (1986). *Narrative psychology: The storied nature of human conduct.* New York: Praeger.

Spera, S. P., Buhrfeind, E. D., & Pennebaker, J. W. (1994). Expressive writing and coping with job loss. *Academy of Management Journal, 37,* 722-733.

White, M., & Epston, D. (1990). *Narrative means to therapeutic ends.* New York: Norton.

INTROSPECTION, FILM REVIEW, AND GROUP DISCUSSION
—*James McGraw*

The exploration of biases is important to the preparation of counselors in training (CITs) (Combs & Gonzalez, 1994). Numerous models of counseling similarly suggest that counselors should strive to suspend their judgments in order to promote relationship building and develop an empathic understanding of the client. This view has received much attention from the multicultural counseling literature (D'Andrea & Daniels, 1991; Pedersen, 1991; Sue, 1991). However, some authors have proposed (Richardson and Molinaro, 1996) that while we have been teaching students about cultural differences, we have neglected to challenge them to uncover their own biases. Student preconceptions may range from tentatively held beliefs, to unquestioned stereotypes, to firmly entrenched biases. Similarly, Carter (1990) has suggested that prior to learning about individuals who are different, prospective counselors should learn about themselves.

A complication of such bias disclosure is worth mentioning. It's exploration of their preconceptions may be complicated, however, by the inherently evaluative nature of counselor training. While CITs are encouraged to explore their shortcomings in the spirit of personal growth, they may restrict their disclosure due to fears that they may be perceived as pathological and that they will then be unable to pursue their desired profession. The anxiety students experience when wanting to appear competent while simultaneously being encouraged to explore their personal shortcomings creates a paradox (Ponterotto & Casas, 1991).

The instructional method described here, Film Stimulated Reflection (FSR), provides both a safe and challenging opportunity for CITs to examine the cultural lenses (including preconceptions and biases) through which they construct knowledge. For numerous semesters, I have used this approach in a Research and Evaluation course to help students contrast naturalistic/qualitative research methods with positivistic/quantitative methods.

Film has been used extensively in education (Reed & Sautter, 1986). I use the medium of film as an instructional strategy for a variety of reasons. A broad selection of concerns and populations can be represented. Multiple viewings are possible. Watching films is an unobtrusive and ethical observation method. Good films can be emotionally powerful and thought-provoking while providing sufficient emotional distance to explore sensitive issues.

Instructors have a wide range of meaningful films to select from. For instance, some critically acclaimed films (and some of my personal favorites) that may engender CIT self-exploration on issues relevant to counseling include: *Love, Valor, and Compassion; Do the Right Thing; Slingblade; The Crossing Guard; Dead Man Walking;* and *The Apostle.*

Objectives

- Promote exploration of preconceptions and biases.

- Normalize CITs' preconceptions that originate from cultural lenses.

- Decrease the resistance that students experience when encountering disowned aspects of self.

- Elicit affective reactions that may lead to increased processing and retention of the learning experience.

- Demonstrate the socially constructed nature of knowledge by allowing CITs an opportunity to dialogue about their personal biases within the context of a diverse peer group.

Description of Activity

This constructivist-based classroom strategy begins with viewing a film clip. The clip serves as a stimulus for introspection and discussion. The general sequence of steps in the instructional process is described below. Each step includes an example of how I used this method in my Research and Evaluation class:

1. The instructor selects a particular film clip to be shown to the CITs. For example, I showed a ten-minute clip of the film *Barfly* have because it provides a realistic depiction of an addiction subculture that is not accessible to most individuals. Based on the autobiography of novelist Charles Bukowski, the film provides an insider's perspective on the life of individuals who drink excessively and live in severe poverty.

2. The CITs write down their preconceptions, prior to viewing the film clip, about individuals who are categorized by some descriptor (such as, a diagnostic category, ethnic group, or religious affiliation, such as schizophrenic, Hispanic, or fundamentalist). For example, in the case of *Barfly*, I present the students with the hypothetical scenario that they "are researchers assigned to unobtrusively observe the social interactions of the so-called 'skid row alcoholic' population." In striving for rigor in observation, students are to document their preconceptions and stereotypes of this group prior to observing the sample of behavior (a film clip).

3. Students watch the film clip and document their observations. For example, in the ten-minute scene from *Barfly*, the main character buys numerous rounds of whiskey for the bar patrons, having recently earned five hundred dollars from the sale of a story he wrote. The variety of social interactions in this scene generates a diversity of student observations and interpretations.

4. Students share the behavioral observations, following the film viewing, that they recorded. I list these observations on the board. For example, student descriptions of the social interactions in *Barfly* have included the following: "grandiosity," "aggressiveness," "no boundaries," "impulsiveness," "loud," "promiscuous," and "self-destructive."

5. Students then share the preconceptions they had previously documented and the instructor writes these on the board next to their list of observations. In the class that used *Barfly*, CITs shared preconceptions of a "skid row alcoholic population" that included such terms as self-destructive, aggressive, irresponsible, and manipulative; we then juxtaposed these descriptions on the board with the list of observations.

6. Students examine the lists of "observations" and "preconceptions" written on the board. The instructor may exercise numerous options to structure this discussion, depending on the material generated by the students. If there is much similarity between the lists, the CITs may be encouraged to consider the degree to which their observations were influenced by their preconceptions. If dissimilarity between the observations and preconceptions is pronounced, the CITs may be asked to describe how they changed their preconceptions. The instructor may also acknowledge and work with the diversity of observations within the group, promote direct interchange among students, and encourage processing of the group discussion itself.

In the *Barfly* example, the students quickly noted the similarity between their lists. A discussion ensued regarding how their preconceptions may have impacted their observations, even though they had attempted to be unbiased in their research. It was also noted that many of the "observations" they verbalized (for example, character grandiosity, or lack of boundaries) were not behaviors per se, but were actually interpretations or even projections.

In one class, during this processing stage, a serendipitous interaction emerged. A student stated that she had recently been to a prestigious convention in a large city. In an affluent hotel bar one evening following the conference, she observed very similar social interactions among nicely dressed, apparently affluent, professional people. Seizing on her example as an opportunity, I invited the class to create a list of corresponding behavioral observations, instead for the professional population of individuals. The students quickly re-framed their perceptions as follows: grandiosity = self-confidence, aggressive = assertive, no boundaries = open, impulsiveness = generous/spontaneous, loud = expressive, promiscuous = flirtatious/liberated, and self-destructive = carefree. Many of the students appeared to have an immediate "aha" about the "constructed" nature of perceptions during this impromptu brainstorming. In subsequent semesters when I have shared this example with students, they appeared to make a vicarious connection with the experience.

7. Generalize the experience to different issues and contexts (such as, diversity issues, commonly held stereotypes). I then encourage students to verbalize how they will explore other unexamined preconceptions and biases. For example, I invite students to reflect on the power that labels such as "alcoholic" have on perceptions, even when people try to remain unbiased. I also ask them to consider the number of times they have heard professionals in educational or clinical settings utilize labels that might bias perception such as "borderline," "schizophrenic," or "sociopath." The students ponder how this use of language might convey information beyond the purpose of efficient clinical communication, how it might stereotype human beings, and how it might become embedded in the jargon of mental health professionals. Lastly, we weave student responses to such questions into a discussion of the assumptions underlying the naturalistic/qualitative model of research, (that is, the favoring of subjective, inductive, multiple realities).

8. The instructor reflects upon the classroom process, and considers follow-up activities and/or modifications for future applications. I also solicit student feedback about the classroom experience, which is an important part of the reflective constructivist process. For example, during my reflections about the course that used *Barfly*, I attended to the palpable shift in the group mood in later sessions when "alcoholics" were discussed. The students seemed to have become more self-aware in their statements and their emotional tone seemed less judgmental and more compassionate. In checking in with the students about their experiences, numerous students indicated that this classroom experience was informative, fun, and meaningful. The exercise had impacted them by reminding them that we all have stereotypes, and that we need to strive continually to address them. We need to be careful about who has the right to judge individuals who are different; criteria used when judgements are made; and judging people differentially depending on their socioeconomic class—"upper class" behaviors may be tolerated, while the same behavior in the "lower classes" may be pathologized.

9. A follow-up discussion after several weeks have passed might allow for additional insights to develop. Topics to broach when revisiting the

FSR could include: "What feelings/thoughts were evoked during the experience?" "What opinions did you censor during the discussion?" "What new insights have emerged relevant to the experience?" "How has your perspective changed since the first viewing?" and "What did you discover about yourself?"

REFERENCES

Carter, R. T. (1990). The relationship between racism and racial identity among White Americans: An exploratory investigation. *Journal of Counseling & Development, 69,* 46-50.

Combs, A. W. & Gonzalez, D. M. (1994*). Helping relationships: Basic concepts for the helping professions.* Boston: Allyn and Bacon.

D'Andrea, M. D., & Daniels, J. (1991). Exploring the different levels of multicultural counseling training in counselor education. *Journal of Counseling & Development, 70(1),* 78-85.

Pedersen, P. P. (1991). Multiculturalism as a generic approach to counseling. *Journal of Counseling & Development, 70*(1), 6-12.

Ponterotto, J. G., & Casas, J. M. (1991*). Handbook of racial/ethnic minority counseling research.* Springfield, IL: Charles C. Thomas.

Reed, S., & Sautter, R. (1986). Video education: Taking a new look at an old technology. *Electronic Learning, 6*(3), 22-27.

Richardson, T. Q., & Molinaro, K. L. (1996). White counselor self-awareness: A prerequisite for developing multicultural competence. *Journal of Counseling & Development, 74*(3), 238-241.

Sue, D. W. (1991). A model for diversity training. *Journal of Counseling & Development, 70*(1), 99-105.

ACTIVITIES FOR INCREASING AWARENESS OF NONVERBAL COMMUNICATION
—Carlotta J. Willis

Most counselor education programs teach verbal communication, nonverbal communication, and human interaction, frequently in the Counseling Skills course. In my teaching, I especially emphasize nonverbal communication because of its dominance in the communication process (Argyle, 1975).

I take an interactional perspective on communication. Such an approach contrasts with the linear, cause-and-effect, or individualistic/diagnostic model for understanding human motivation and behavior that is common in most literature on nonverbal communication. Norton and Brenders (1996) presented a description of communication that reflects this shift from a linear to contextual understanding. I use three of their foundational constructs to enhance students' understanding of the subjective interpretation of nonverbal communication (italics ours). These constructs are the following:

- A person fills in premises in a way that makes sense to the self. (*The Law of Enthymematic Communication*, p. xviii)[1]

- Communication is a process in which the individual interactively supplies premises to make sense out of a message. (p. xvii)

- As a person completes an enthymeme regarding information from the other, a soft boundary is created that focuses interpretations. A communicative frame emerges that provides a more or less reliable interpretive guide. Inferences are made about intentions, meaning, and implications of what is said [or not said, as the case may be]. (p.44)

The advantage of the constructivist approach to teaching is that students' experiences are valued and are incorporated into an expanded notion of learning. Thus instructors can build on their students' abilities, rather than assuming a level of competence or incompetence. Consistent with that participatory and individualized vein, I prefer to weave the course material into group discussion, generated by student questions or observations, rather than to deliver a packaged lecture on the subject.

The following exercises can be used together as a complete workshop that is aimed at developing skill in, and awareness of nonverbal communication. Alternatively, each can be used individually to supplement exploration of related topics. The overall objective of the experiential exercises is to elicit the student's own thinking and to build a base for expansion and additional learning and reflection.

CLASSROOM EXPERIENCES

Activity One: Introducing the Enthymematic Process through Viewing an Interaction

During this exercise, students become aware of the personal associations and behavioral evidence used in constructing impressions of people's behavior and relationships. I show a sequence from the British film, *Secrets and Lies* (Leigh, 1996), and ask students to observe the couple's interaction. I use the exercise at the beginning of the course, prior to any lecture on communication, to demonstrate the wealth of knowledge that students already possess about communication.

The film excerpt begins with Monica Purley vacuuming the hallway, right behind the front door. Maurice, her husband, is coming home at dinner time. As he enters the home he bumps into Monica, who is very upset and edgy. The following interchange[2] takes place between them:

She: "What do you think you're doing?"

He: "Sorry?"

She: "Didn't you hear me? . . . Mind, out of the way."
(He tries to kiss her. She pushes him off. He goes into the kitchen and gets a bottle of wine out of the refrigerator, and looks back at her.)

He: "Want a drink?"

She: "What? If I want a drink, I'll get it myself, thank you."
(He puts the bottle back. She puts the vacuum cleaner away, as he watches.)
"Since when was Hoovering a spectator sport?"
(She walks into the kitchen. He reaches for a glass.)

She: "Can I have a glass too please."

He: "I thought you weren't. . . ."

She: "I changed my mind, I'm having milk."
(He hands her a wine glass.)
"Not a wine glass. Give me a high ball. You don't put milk in a wine glass."

He: "There you go."

She: "Thank you."

He: "How. . . (unclear what is said)?"

She: "Meaning?"

He: "Nothing. Have a good day, did you?"

She: "Scintillating."
      (She opens and shuts several cabinet doors in the kitchen and stares into the open oven).
      "Suppose you'll be starving as usual."

He: "A little bit peckish, yeah."
      (They both sit at the table; she drinks her milk.)
      "You want me to do something?"

She: "Like what?"

He: "Anything you like."

She: "No, I bloody well wouldn't."

He: "Fair enough."
      (She gets up and begins opening and slamming doors again.)

She: "All right then. There's the fridge. There's the freezer. There is the hop [stove]. There's a recipe book. Help yourself. And don't make a mess."
      (She exits, then returns.)
      "Unless you fancy a take-away?"
      (He smiles. She begins crying, leaves and shuts the kitchen door.)

After watching the clip twice, I ask the class to discuss in small groups the following questions: What was going on? How did you come to that conclusion? What behavioral data are you using to construct this scenario? On what in your own history and experience are you basing your ideas?

Each group reports to the class. During the reports and the ensuing discussion, no definite conclusions are drawn because the film interaction has multiple interpretations, even within the film's story. Using this particular clip allows the students to explore both their own prejudices and how they use their own personal histories to punctuate a sequence. As the discussion progresses, I highlight the basic parameters of communications and, in particular, nonverbal communication. Students almost always mention as evidence for their interpretations, the specific communicational behaviors used, such as tone of voice, rate of speech, word choice, body movements, facial expression, and sequence of behaviors. I can easily weave research on nonverbal communication and the enthymematic process into such a discussion. The overall exercise takes forty-five minutes to an hour, depending on how much didactic material on communication is presented.

Activity Two: The Impact of the Enthymematic Process on Style

I illustrate how the communicational dimensions of content and style influence each other by using a video example from Beavers' (1992) *Family Assessment* video series. In this sequence of tapes, two role-played families use virtually the same script, but a different actor plays the mother in the second role play. We discuss the different communication styles of the two "mothers," and students identify the effect of the different styles on their own enthymematic process. This exercise demonstrates the large difference made by subtle behavioral changes and the variability of interpretation depending on the student's own cultural, familial, and historical contexts. The same objective might be reached by having students conduct parallel role plays based on prepared scripts. The scripts could consist of the same dialogues but might use different motivations, classes, genders, and cultural roles. Each group can videotape its version, and the versions could be compared as above.

Activity Three: Family of Origin Communication Styles

This exercise illustrates the student's own family of origin interactional patterns and introduces students to the varieties of such patterns. The exercise continues, demonstrating the contextual aspects of interpreting behavior and further illustrating the enthymematic process.

The exercise progresses as follows. I ask students, before the session, to reflect on their family of origin's communicational patterns. During the session, I cluster the class into like groups (using ethnicity, region, religion, functional/dysfunctional patterns, or other clusters that class members develop for themselves and are comfortable with) to discuss the following questions: "How would you know if your mother or father were sad, angry, proud, happy...etc.?" "How were disagreements handled?" "How was closeness or distance expressed?" "How was the family hierarchy maintained?" "How were gender roles assigned?" "What patterns seem to vary with culture?"

Each group typically organizes and presents the material in its own way. The process can be very meaningful and moving as students gain insight into each others' contexts. For example, students have revealed the patterns of violence and shame in alcoholic and abusive families and the impact of these patterns on their current enthymematic processes. Awareness of such patterns is very important for both the group of students from such families and the students from more open and direct families. Although the instructor also weaves research and literature into the discussion, hearing their fellow students' stories remains the most powerful learning experience. It opens up the varieties of family behavior more meaningfully than could any textbook description of dysfunctional family communication patterns.

Activity Four: Co-Created Processes in Kinesic Behavior

Students observe dyadic nonverbal behavior in the following exercise in order to understand the co-created, contextual nature of nonverbal communication. Most counselor training in nonverbal communication either relies on relatively static postures (forward lean, eye contact, matched body position) or on observation of the client's behavior in isolation (Okun, 1997). Ivey's more recent work (1994) discusses movement synchrony and the more subtle interplay between counselor and client. However, he offers little advice about how to observe such behavior or how to train counselors to produce it. I devised the *Index of Nonverbal Coordination* (Willis, 1989), based on the method of "Labanalysis" (Bartenieff, 1980), to structure observations of mutual kinesic coordination.

Mutual kinesic coordination is a process through which people adjust their body movements to EACH OTHER in a synchronous pattern. As a clinician, I use my awareness of nonverbal mutuality as a process observation skill and as a self-monitoring, self-awareness skill to gauge my connection with a client. I do not try to artificially mirror the client, but rather I observe the natural flow of the behavior and use it as data for clinical hypothesis testing and for assessing the working relationship between myself and my clients. By focusing in class on the mutuality of nonverbal behavior, we reinforce the students' understanding of the nonverbal aspects of joining, empathy, and relational counseling.

I begin this exercise by defining and demonstrating the categories of mutual behavior: Shared Position, Rhythmic Coordination, Similarity of Shape, Dynamic Similarity, Echoing, Subtle Attunement, Heightened Similarity, and a global category—Kinesic Coordination (Willis, 1989; see appendix for working definitions). I also discuss and demonstrate a corresponding verbal process—speech accommodation—in which speakers synchronize speech rate, pitch, and other factors during an interchange (Street & Giles, 1982). These categories help students identify and understand the dynamic interplay of nonverbal and verbal coordination between two persons. This awareness sensitizes them to the effect that their own nonverbal behavior may have on an interaction and the effect that that of others may have on them.

After I discuss and demonstrate these mutual behaviors, students divide into groups of four to practice and identify mutual nonverbal coordination. Two students have a conversation while the other two observe and videotape the process. All four students then observe the video and try to pick out examples of such coordination. The dyads then switch and repeat the process. Each group of four brings an example back to the large group to demonstrate their learning.

This exercise can be done in an hour and a half, although more time can be spent looking at the tapes and sharing discoveries if desired. Frequently, I also ask students to observe dyads in naturalistic settings after they have established their familiarity with the concepts during class. They may additionally keep an observational journal for a few weeks and write essays about their learnings.

CONCLUSION

By completing this series of exercises, students develop a greater awareness of their own communication patterns, of the interactional aspects of communication, and of the enthymematic process. The frame of context and enthymematic construction is kept as a central focus. Students are continually encouraged to make their own enthymematic process overt by exploring their assumptions and meanings and understanding their own communicational contexts. As a part of each exercise, the contexts of culture, gender, situation, and relationships are considered. The old model of a one-to-one correspondence between communicational behavior and meaning is reevaluated through reflection and experience.

NOTES

1. Funk and Wagnalls *Standard College Dictionary* defines an "enthymeme" as "an argument in which the conclusion or one of the premises is not stated." It comes from the Greek "en" or "in" and "thymos" or "mind."

2. The dialogue is quoted from the video (Fox Video: October Films, 1996) and is approximate, used here for demonstration purposes.

APPENDIX

Definitions of the Nonverbal Coordination Categories

Shared Position: The interactants share similar or identical positions with their upper and lower bodies. They need not take the positions at the same time; they need only be in the same or similar positions during the observation period. The positions may be mirrored (i.e., right leg of one is in the position of the left leg of the other) or on the same side of the body (right leg of one is in the position of the right leg of the other). Basic body positions are considered, not the gestures accompanying of those positions.

Rhythmic Coordination: The interactants seem to move in similar rhythmic patterns as if sharing the same tempo. Their movement need not be exactly alike, nor with the same body part, but rather it should have a complementarity or coordination, a similar tempo. The focus is on the timing in their interaction.

Echoing: A movement is initiated by one person and is then replicated either in exact, expanded, or abbreviated form, usually within seconds of the original movement. It need not be with the same body part, but should have the same or similar rhythm, action, or quality.

Dynamic Similarity: The interactants move with a similar movement quality. They seem to match each other in dynamic style or seem to be expressing the same energy and feeling. Examples of movement quality might be: forceful or soft emphasis, precision or vagueness of gesture, tight or fluid style, quick or slow gestures.

Similarity of Shape: The interactants make similar shapes in space. Their gestures could share similar curves, angles, straight lines, arcs, or twists. The shapes could be made with any body part, although most of the shapes will be made in hand gestures. They need not be made at the same time, as long as it is clear that the shapes are the same.

Subtle Attunement: The interactants have small movement interchanges with each other through breath and muscle patterns of holding and release. Their coordination can be seen on a muscular level or through very tiny movements, such as small hand motions, breathing patterns, sighs, or pauses.

Heightened Synchrony: A moment when interactants move exactly alike at precisely the same time. They move in simultaneous and identical patterns of gesture, postural shift, and/or action. Neither seems to lead or follow. The key is that the movement be virtually identical in timing, quality, and body part, although it need not involve the whole body. The moments may be very small or quick, and the feeling is of great togetherness of action. These are rare moments.

Kinesic Coordination: This remaining category is a global category, encompassing behaviors from all the above categories. The interactants appear to be "in sync" with one another. Their movements are coordinated and interlinked as if they were dancing together. This category takes into account all the previous aspects of shared position, rhythmic coordination, echoing, dynamic similarity, similarity of shape, and heightened synchrony.

REFERENCES

Argyle, M. (1975). *Bodily communication*. New York: International University Press, Inc.

Bartenieff, I. (with Lewis, D.) (1980). *Body movement: Coping with the environment*. New York: Gordon and Breach.

Beavers, W. R. (1992). *Family* assessment. New York: Norton & Co.

Beavers, W. R. & Hampson, R. B. (1990). *Successful families: Assessment and intervention*. New York: Norton & Co.

Ivey, A. (1994). *Intentional interviewing and counseling: Facilitating client development in a multicultural society*. Pacific Grove: CA: Brooks-Cole.

Leigh, M. (1996). *Secrets and lies* [Film, available on video]. London: October Films, Fox Video.

Norton, R. and Brenders, D. (1996). *Communication and consequences: Laws of interaction*. Mahwah, NJ: Lawrence Erlbaum Associates.

Okun, B. F. (1997). *Effective helping*. Pacific Grove, CA: Brooks/Cole.

Street R. L., & Giles, H. (1982). Speech accommodation theory: A social cognitive approach to language and speech behavior. In M. E. Roloff & C. R. Berger (Eds.), *Social cognition and communication*, (pp. 193-226). Beverly Hills, CA: Sage Publishing.

Willis, C. J.(1989). The measurement of mutual nonverbal coordination in the psychotherapeutic process: An exploratory study of the development of an index for clinical use. Unpublished doctoral dissertation. University of Massachusetts, Amherst.

Recommended Reading for Classroom Exercises

Bennett, M. J., & Stewarts, E. C. (1991). *American cultural patterns*. Yarmouth, ME: Intercultural Press, Inc.

Ekman, P. (1993). Facial expression and emotion. *American Psychologist, 48(4)*, 384-391.

Gardner, H. (1993). *Multiple intelligences: The theory in practice*. New York: Basic Books.

Jorgenson, J. (1995). Re-relationalizing rapport in interpersonal setting. In W. Leeds-Hurwitz (Ed.), *Social approaches to communication*, pp.155-170. New York: Guilford Press.

Norton, R. and Brenders, D. (1996). *Communication and consequences: Laws of interaction*. Mahwah, NJ: Lawrence Erlbaum Associates.

Tannen, D. (1993). The relativity of linguistic strategies: Rethinking power and solidarity in gender and dominance. In D. Tannen, *Gender and Conversational Interaction*, pp.165-188. New York: Oxford University Press.

Watzlawick, P., Babelas, J. B., & Jackson, D. D. (1967). *Pragmatics of human communication*. New York: Norton & Co.

THE "ARCHEOLOGICAL DIG" EXERCISE: IDENTIFYING PERSONAL HYPOTHESES AND UNCOVERING BIASES ABOUT CLIENTS
—Lois Benishek

I have vivid recollections of a class discussion that was initiated by one of my first practicum instructors. She asked us, "Is counseling value-free?" Being both naive and having a strong need to demonstrate that I was a good, conscientious student, I was the first to respond to her question. I answered with a resounding, "Yes!" My pride, however, was soon tempered by the instructor's ever-so-careful prompting about how we often unknowingly bring our personal biases into many aspects of our professional lives.

Counseling, for better or worse, is not value-free. But in order to ensure that we do not intentionally or unintentionally impose our values on our clients, it is imperative that we become aware of them, that we be able to "see" them when they are present. Failing to do so could hinder client growth or result in clients not receiving the most beneficial type of mental health treatment.

A task typically performed by counselors in which biases can become apparent is that of diagnosing clients. Many professionals in counseling-related fields have taken issue with this labeling process for philosophical and/or political reasons. They have either recommended avoiding diagnoses (Szasz, 1970) or have recommended finding ways to minimize the negative effects associated with diagnosis (Levy, 1981; Morrow & Deidan, 1992; Parker, Georgaca, Harper, McLaughlin, & Stowell-Smith, 1997). However, the task of diagnosis is not likely to go away soon, because, fortunately or unfortunately, managed care groups and other insurance organizations are intent on requiring counselors to diagnose clients. These organizations use diagnoses to justify clients receiving insurance coverage for their mental health needs, thus ensuring that counselors receive monetary reimbursement for the services they provide.

Given that counselors can no longer avoid diagnosing their clients, they must become aware of those times when their biases and stereotypes enter the diagnostic process. Failure to do so may result in clients being diagnosed as more dysfunctional than they actually are. Such misdiagnosis may occur more often when counselors are unaware of how their own unique life experiences color and distort the lenses through which perceive their clients.

The Archeological Dig exercise increases counselor trainees' awareness of how their life histories impact their perceptions of clients, which, in turn, may influence how they diagnose those clients. The "Dig" helps trainees begin to make explicit their previously implicit cognitions about clients. With this heightened knowledge, students then "unearth" existing biases and stereotypes about which they may not have had knowledge prior to participating in this exercise.

The "Dig" is useful in a number of ways. First, the exercise takes place in a safe, non-threatening learning environment, an environment that encourages students to freely express stereotypical responses: racist thoughts, class biases, or sexist attitudes that most of them have been socialized not to admit. The instructor explicitly states that no response expressed in class will be attacked or devalued and that students will not be penalized for expressing thoughts that are not "politically correct."

Second, the "digging" process results in greater personal and professional awareness. The self-reflectiveness of the activity encourages counselors to search for the origins of their biases and stereotypes and to begin to understand how their life histories and contexts have colored the lenses through which they see their clients. For instance, a trainee is encouraged to recognize that being raised in an affluent family, coupled with a lack of interaction with working class or poor people, has led her to develop a bias that these individuals aren't intelligent or don't have good work ethics.

Finally, this exercise can be used in many undergraduate and graduate courses. In addition to using it in courses pertaining to psychopathology and diagnosis, the "dig" can be integrated into coursework in assessment, multicultural counseling, counseling theories, and personality theories (normal personality development). Instructors may also use it in research-related courses in which students develop research questions and hypotheses as a part of completing their theses or dissertations. The exercise helps students to begin to recognize that research is not value-free. Personal biases underlie the types of research questions and hypotheses that are generated, as well as how the results are interpreted.

"Dig" Objectives

- to enhance student counselors' diagnostic skills, and

- to help students identify biases and stereotypes they they may inadvertently impose on their clients when involved in diagnostic and/or counseling activities.

Description of the Activity

Step 1. Select a 4-6 minute segment of any videotape which has one person as its primary focus. The segment should provide a substantial number of non-verbal and verbal behaviors. The individual should exhibit enough symptoms to warrant a DSM-IV diagnosis or have enough characteristics to suggest the possible presence of a diagnosis. Although films and videotapes from popular media may be used, the DSM-IV videotapes published by the American Psychiatric Association also work well. The "Jerry" vignette (based on DSM-III-R criteria) usually elicits a variety of stereotypes. Counselor trainees often erroneously hypothesize that "Jerry" is a depressed, substance abusing gay man.

Step 2. Provide the counselor trainees with the following directions: "You are about to view a brief segment of a videotape. Simply watch the videotape and record (on paper) your responses to the sentence stems that I am about to give you. Write down as many responses as you can based on any thoughts that happen to pop into your head. There are no right or wrong responses. The stems I want you to respond to are the following:

'I think...[what, about this person?].' [For example, 'I think this person is suicidal.']

'I wonder if this person is ... [what?]?' [For example, 'I wonder if this person is nervous.']"

This begins the process of getting counselors to generate viable working hypotheses about the individual in the videotape. The open-ended nature of the prompts allows an opportunity for potential biases and stereotypes to become "unearthed."

Step 3. Show about one minute of the videotape and stop the video recorder. Ask the counselor trainees to generate a list of responses (working hypotheses) about the person they have just observed. Allow them time to write down their responses and then ask them to share those responses with the class. Do not evaluate their responses. Simply write them on the chalkboard, and ask each student to provide a justification for his or her statements (such as, how they came to view or construct their perceptions of the person in that particular way).

Step 4. Play another one or two brief segments of the videotape, asking the counselor trainees to generate more responses to the stems. Continue this process until the students have exhausted their responses. Conflicting responses often emerge by the end of this process. Grouping students' responses into logical categories will help to identify common themes as well as discrepant thoughts about the individual who was just observed.

Step 5. After generating an exhaustive list of responses (hypotheses), ask the counselor trainees what DSM-IV diagnosis they would assign to this person. Have the students provide a rationale for their decision. Ask other students in the class to support or counter the diagnoses that are being generated (for example, "Marissa would diagnosis the person as having a Major Depressive Disorder. Charles would assign a diagnosis of Schizoid Personality Disorder. Celine hypothesizes that the person is experiencing Social Phobia. In what ways do these diagnoses make sense? In what ways don't they make sense?"). Following this discussion, you can provide the students with the DSM-IV diagnosis that you believe best fits this individual.

Step 6. It is important for the instructor to remember that providing the counselor trainees with the DSM-IV diagnosis is only the secondary purpose of this activity. The primary purpose is to help the trainees to gain insight into the biases that they bring to the diagnostic process. One way to start this primary work is to shift the focus of the class to a discussion of the following: (a) How we, as a society, have constructed these diagnostic categories. For example discuss the writings of Thomas Szasz (1961, 1970) and others such as Kirk & Kutchins (1992). Note how some diagnoses have been deleted from the various versions of the DSM over time, not without controversy, because society no longer considers those behaviors to be "abnormal" or "dysfunctional" (Gonsoriek, 1991). Discuss how efforts are being made to recognize that 'normal' reactions expressed in certain cultural groups are misperceived as 'abnormal' by the predominant culture (Mezzich, 1995). (b) How we, as a society and as individuals, might view the person on the videotape differently if (s)he were of another sex, race/ethnicity, class.

Step 7. The instructor can use this information as the segue into a discussion about how our personal histories, biases, and stereotypes influence our constructions of clients and how this can inadvertently harm our clients. This instructor might say:

Notice how we generated a broad range of working hypotheses about this person today. Also, notice how we generated more than one diagnosis for this person and we had a rationale for each of them. How is it that we all observed the same individual for the same amount of time and, yet, our working hypotheses about this person were so different?

Pause for a minute and think about your life history and your present life context. How did they affect your view of this person? How did they impact your construction of who this person was and the diagnosis you thought was most appropriate for them?

In what ways might your life history and life context help you to be a more effective diagnostician and counselor? In what ways, might it hinder you? How can we, as counseling professionals, help one another to become more aware of our biases and ways in which we might impose them in a harmful way upon our clients?

Breaking through the Rocks and Hitting Paydirt

Some students are comfortable generating and verbalizing "risky" hypotheses about the person they observe; others are not. The degree of hesitancy or defensiveness varies based on the sensitivity of the content presented in the videotape, the trainee's degree of self-awareness and self-confidence, and the level of trust and cohesiveness that exists among the counselor trainees and the instructor. Resistance to self-exploration might be addressed in one of two ways. First, the instructor can actively model "more threatening," "riskier," or less "politically correct" statements about her or his impressions of the individual on the videotape (for example, "I think Jerry is gay."). This implicitly reconfirms the statement made earlier by the instructor that there are no wrong responses. It also communicates that all responses are worthy of consideration and further exploration. A second way to engage counselor trainees in more open and genuine dialogue is to begin with a less threatening segment of a videotape, one that is likely to "uncover" less risky biases. For instance, students may feel more comfortable stating that they think the person is an alcoholic than that (s)he is gay. Over time, the instructor can move into more sensitive content areas.

Counselor trainees may also begin to "unearth" their implicit assumptions about a given client by observing and critiquing their own videotaped diagnostic and counseling sessions. Awareness may emerge in dialogues with their supervisor and/or classmates about (a) the origin of the biases, (b) the extent to which the biases impact how they interact with the client in the session, and (c) the ramifications of that interaction for the clients' progress in counseling.

REFERENCES

Gonsoriek, J. C. (1991). The empirical basis for the demise of the illness model of homosexuality. In J. Gonsiorek and J. Weinrich (Eds.). *Homosexuality: Research implications for public policy*, (pp. 115-136). Newbury Park, CA: Sage Publications.

Kirk, S. A., & Kutchins, H. (1992). *The selling of the DSM: The rhetoric of science in psychiatry*. New York: Aldine De Gruyter.

Levy, C. S. (1981). Labeling: The social worker's responsibility. *Social Casework, 62*, 332-342.

Mezzich, J. E. (1995). Cultural formulation and comprehensive diagnosis. *The Psychiatric Clinics of North America, 18*, 649-657.

Morrow, K. A., & Deidan, C. T. (1992). Bias in the counseling process: How to recognize and avoid it. *Journal of Counseling and Development, 70*, 571-577.

Parker, I., Georgaca, E., Harper, D., McLaughlin, T., & Stowell-Smith, M. (1997). *Deconstructing psychopathology*. Thousand Oaks, CA: Sage Publications.

Szasz, T. S. (1961). *The myth of mental illness: Foundations of a theory of human conduct*. New York: Hober-Harper.

Szasz, T. S. (1970). Psychiatric classification as a strategy of personal constraint. In T. S. Szasz, *Ideology and insanity: Essays on the psychiatric dehumanization of man*, (pp. 190-217). Garden City, NY: Anchor Books.

4

Activities for Increasing Multicultural Awareness

Garrett McAuliffe, Marilyn J. Montgomery, Raquel Contreras,

Aretha Faye Marbley, William M. Kurtines, and Karen Eriksen

WALT WHITMAN'S CHALLENGE:
THE SELF-AUTHORIZING ACTIVITY
—Garrett McAuliffe

We lack development-enhancing interventions. Despite there being many Piagetian-based cognitive, or "constructive" developmental theories, there are few stars to guide educators in the direction of influencing development. And yet influence is our aim. One major goal of counselor education is to help future counselors to become more empathic, self-aware, and socially critical. All of these are characteristic of a developmental shift from so-called conformist thinking to a more autonomous, "self-authorizing" capacity (Belenky, Clinchy, Goldberger, and Tarule; 1986; Kegan, 1994; Loevinger, 1976). Educators aim to produce counselors who are autonomous and interdependent, counselors who can weigh evidence for decisions, rather than relying solely on knowledge received from authorities.

Much developmental instruction already occurs, whether it goes by that label or not. For example, we ask students to choose and defend a preferred counseling theory, and we ask them to develop their own case conceptualizations in practica and internships. However, merely completing these assignments does not necessarily awaken students to their current world view, nor does it instigate cross-context changes in their ways of knowing. If students are to shift from a generally "conformist" (Loevinger,

1976), or "received" mode for knowing (Belenky, Clinchy, Goldberger, and Tarule, 1986), to a more self-authorizing (Kegan, 1994) or procedural one (Belenky et al., 1986), they must confront such questions as, "*How* did I come to consider this theory/intervention/case conceptualization to be good/valuable/important?" and more generally, "What do I want to decide, *based on the careful weighing of evidence*, at this time?" The "Self-Authorizing Activity" activity presented here challenges students to consider the sources of their current knowing, to reconsider the sources that they wish to rely on, to rethink the content of their beliefs, and to decide for themselves what they understand to be good, important, and valuable.

The Self-Authorizing Activity utilizes nineteenth-century American poet Walt Whitman's "manifesto," from his *Leaves of Grass* (1855/1969) to instigate such change. Whitman wrote:

This is what you should do: love the earth and sun and the animals, despise riches, give alms to everyone that asks, stand up for the stupid and crazy, devote your income and labor to others, hate tyrants, argue not concerning God, have patience and indulgence toward the people, take off your hat to nothing known or unknown or to any man [sic] or number of men…**re-examine all you have been told at school or church or in any book** [boldface mine], dismiss what insults your own soul, and your very flesh shall be a great poem. (p. 1968).

The hyperbole of his polemic aside, Whitman challenges us to decide for ourselves what matters. I quote the sentence "Re-examine all you have been told at school or church or in any book" for this exercise. As I interpret it, the phrase challenges students to step back from their cultures, to de-center from inherited custom, in favor of actively choosing their positions on matters of importance.

This shift from knee-jerk conformity and/or rampant relativism to a commitment to evidence-sifting procedures for knowing is the central aim of liberal arts education, although our students often arrive in counselor education programs without such an education or epistemology (Fong, Borders, Ethington, & Pitts, 1997; Lovell, 1999; Neukrug & McAuliffe, 1993).

Counselor education may itself not promote students' further epistemelogical development, for it is a very practical enterprise; we may eschew critical reflection in favor of technical training. The "Self-Authorizing Activity" aims to augment our very practical training by asking students to become "critical," to confront their dearest beliefs and habits, and to consider how a currently held belief or doctrine or "truth" might be otherwise. Such a "de-centering" allows culture to be treated as a story, a story that we have written (albeit most times unconsciously), one that we can become conscious of, and one that we can rewrite. No longer is it necessary to abide forever in inherited and perhaps imprisoning stories. The following activity thus confronts ethnocentrism and any other essentialist dogma that students might have inherited and thus taken for granted.

Such a confrontation can be disturbing and over-challenging to conformity-reliant students. For the identity-foreclosed student, this exercise is likely to be beyond their capacity. We must tread softly on these students' sacred customs by allowing them to initially name relatively safe notions for deconstruction. Thereby we merely introduce the possibility of deciding for oneself, through smaller, less-threatening matters, such as food customs and "proper" language and etiquette. We can instigate gently, but we cannot shrink from the challenge. Others who are "ready" for such challenges see the activity as an invitation to extend their self-authorizing inclinations further.

Objectives

- To trigger a shift in students' ways of knowing toward self-authorizing or independent thinking.

- To have students deconstruct culturally based attitudes, beliefs, and behaviors so that a more social constructionist and multicultural position might be achieved.

Description of the Activity

The instructor distributes the two-page worksheet that is contained in the Appendix, reads the directions and the rationale on the first page of the worksheet, and then reads the Whitman segment. On the second page, students privately name six beliefs, manners, behaviors, or attitudes that they have inherited from home, religion, or school (two from each). In the past, students have listed such items as, "Men must be the primary breadwinner," "Restraint in all things is important," "I must go to church every Sunday," "Sex before marriage is a sin," and "Homosexual behavior is abhorrent." Students next take time to privately name an alternate or contrary position for each of the six. Finally, they decide which of the two positions they would be inclined toward if they were challenged to independently provide (of home, religion, or school) evidence for the position.

In small groups of four or five, students spend a half-hour discussing each of their positions. They report to the large group on the trends, common elements, differences, and the feelings that emerged during the discussion.

After the large-group reports are finished, the instructor leads a discussion on how we come by our beliefs. She or he might introduce ethnocentrism at this time, as well as the potential dangers and benefits of conformity and adherence to tradition. The instructor might introduce some examples of the problems of blind conformity, such as blindness to bias, oppression, and injustice (such as, racial segregation and inequality). Conformist thinking can also support subtle exclusions with terrible consequences (gay and lesbian youth suicide, isolation and attrition from schools due to race or ethnicity). The instructor may balance this discussion with a reminder of the positive roles that tradition can serve in society. For instance, historically, children have not had such a difficult time determining their life's careers, as tradition usually held that they followed in their father's footsteps. People also find comfort in the traditions and rituals of their churches in times of distress and grieving. Such a discussion offers support and understanding to students who find comfort in conforming to certain traditions.

Instructors may refer back to this activity in other discussions during the semester, especially if cognitive developmental issues are presented in the course. In the Social and Cultural Issues or Multicultural Counseling course, the activity can be linked to bias, racism, and ethnocentrism, thus offering a personalized way of engaging students in rethinking the source and the content of their beliefs and manners.

CONCLUSION

One final note of moderation: Such a personal revolution in one's general way of thinking is not quickly nor easily achieved. Evidence (Kegan, 1994) points to the need for, at a minimum, a year of testing, doubting, falling "back," trying out, pondering, listening, and overreacting before a full change in epistemological position takes place and a new way of knowing is consistently used. But once a person gives up an essentialist foundation, she or he is unlikely to return to the automatic allegiances, and prejudices, of conformist thinking. She might be heard proclaiming, in the words of Whitman's contemporary, Ralph Waldo Emerson, "What *I* must do is all that concerns me, not what the people think." Perhaps the Self-Authorizing Activity can help the future counselor give herself permission to discover what she must do.

REFERENCES

Belenky, M., Clinchy, B., Goldberger, N., & Tarule, J. (1986). *Women's ways of knowing*. New York: Basic Books.

Fong, M. L., Borders, L. D., Ethington, C. A., & Pitts, J. H. (1997). Becoming a counselor: A longitudinal study of student cognitive development. *Counselor Education and Supervision, 27,* 100-114.

Kegan, R. (1994). *In over our heads: The mental demands of modern life.* Cambridge: Harvard University Press.

Loevinger, J. (1976). *Ego development: Conceptions and theories.* San Francisco: Jossey-Bass.

Lovell, C. (1999). Empathic-cognitive development in students of counseling. *Journal of Adult Development, 6* (4), 195-203.

Neukrug, E. S., & McAuliffe, G. J. (1993). Cognitive development and human service education. *Human Service Education,13,* 13-26.

Whitman, W. (1855/1969). Preface to the 1855 Edition of *Leaves of Grass.* In H. Meserole, W. Sutton, & B. Weber (Eds.), *American literature: Tradition and innovation.* Lexington, MA: D.C. Heath.

APPENDIX

The "Walt Whitman" Activity: A Challenge to "Self-Authorize"

Designed by Garrett McAuliffe, Old Dominion University

Goals:

To help move individuals toward more "independent"* or "autonomous" thinking.

To help individuals construct their own meanings and standards, rather than being ethnocentrically bound to one cultural perspective or other inherited world views.

(* Note: "Independence" does not mean separateness from others or lack of community commitment.)

Walt Whitman, the nineteenth-century American writer, wrote, in *Leaves of Grass*:

"Re-examine all you have been told at school or church [or at home] or in any book, dismiss what insults your own soul, and your very flesh shall be a great poem."

That **"poem"** might be translated as the "self-authorizing self," the you who decides for yourself (as much as that is possible, since we are always "in" the social context. Thus Whitman encourages us to have an *independent vision* of what we believe and value, and how we act, a vision based on careful consideration of what matters to us, a vision that is separate from the supposed "givens" of culture. (That, in itself, is a very American cultural value!). In this vision of the self-authorizing person, conventions are treated as social constructions, ones that can be deconstructed for their value in a particular historical, political, or cultural context. They are subject to re-thinking based on consideration of evidence: Do they work? Do they help? Whom do they serve?

In order to start, or continue, on the path to "self-authorizing," (vs. relying on common beliefs and conventions for living), try this activity:

1. On the attached form, under "Inherited Beliefs," name two beliefs, "truths," standards, manners, customs, or behaviors that you have been taught for each category (for example, school, religion, home). Such customs are often around interpersonal behavior, manners, family structures and behaviors, gender roles, attitudes toward other races or ethnic groups, sexual behavior, alternate sexual orientations, career, patriotism, loyalties, religious notions, God, "true" faith, the good life, material goods, the place of work vs. leisure. You can also use the social group memberships, or "GARREACS," as stimuli for thinking about beliefs and behaviors you have inherited. Take a risk: name some strong, deep beliefs that you hold absolutely about how things should be, or about what is true and right. You can also name some "lighter" customs.

2. Then, under the second column, "Alternate," write an alternative behavior, custom, or belief, one that challenges the inherited one ("The gay and lesbian sexual orientation is natural and I support and appreciate the presence of gay and lesbian people in our community." or "Atheism is not the only viable or valuable belief system; belief in God is important for many people and can be a positive force.")

3. Then think about each initial inherited belief and each alternative belief, and decide on the one that you might currently consider, based on re-thinking your initial way of coming to know it. What current evidence can you gather for your custom or belief? Write that evidence in the third column, "Current Choice and Evidence." Remember, you can re-affirm, modify, or reject your inherited beliefs based on evidence. You need not necessarily reject them; you can instead reclaim them in a new way, perhaps as "principles," not as rigid rules. Also, reconsidering inherited conventions cannot necessarily occur in the short time it takes to do this exercise. Consider this to be a beginning of a "self-authorizing" way of knowing ("procedural knowing').

4. Finally, on the back of the page, write a paragraph on your reaction to doing this activity—your feelings and thoughts.

Inherited Beliefs/Customs	Alternate	Current Choice and Evidence

(For example, regarding manners, gender roles, "proper" behavior, morals, sexual orientation, sexual behavior, career, work, patriotism, rules, "others," family structure, race, religion.)

School

1.

2.

Religion

1.

2.

Home

1.

2.

IDENTIFYING CULTURAL GROUP MEMBERSHIPS:
AN INTRODUCTORY ACTIVITY
—Garrett McAuliffe

A promising and broad context for framing multicultural thinking is to link it to the *social constructionist* meta-theory. Social constructionism has brought a multi-perspectival, reflective, critical impulse to social science and counseling practice. It is integral to much feminist theory, social psychology, and post-modern philosophy. Its relationship to counselor education has been described more extensively elsewhere (for example, McAuliffe & Lovell, 2000; Sexton & Griffin, 1997). Most simply put, in the social constructionist frame the focus is on the pervasive influence of the language and the communities that we are always "in" for our meaning-making. Stated differently, the "social" is always in the individual, and vice-versa. Our names, our notions of the good life, our dialects, our aspirations, are all inseparable from the cultures that create us.

Our relationship to the social context may not be uniform, however. The so-called *constructive developmentalists* (Belenky, Clinchy, Goldberger, and Tarule; 1986; Kegan, 1994; Loevinger, 1976) suggest that we might be more or less "free" of the social surround. They emphasize our evolving "relationships to" the social. One dimension of the social is culture. An implication of constructive developmental theory is that humans can have more or less embeddedness in their cultures; they can have varying relationships to them. In constructivist terms, we can "deconstruct" our experience of culture.

Both types of constructivism can be introduced to students in a personalized, flexible, experiential fashion in the following activity. The exercise introduces at least eight "cultural group memberships" to students. Through it, students come to recognize the influence of these groups on their lives and can challenge the traditional Western notion of the universal, decontextualized autonomous self. In this way, the activity may trigger the beginning of a paradigm shift for students.

"Naming" their cultural affiliations is only the beginning of the exercise, however. In its second phase students are asked to speculate on the status and power differences among cultural groups and the impact of those differences both on individual cultural groups and on the larger society. Students thus can begin to uncover the varying statuses and privileges that are accorded to different cultural groups. Similarly, in this second phase, students explore how power hierarchies change depending on the time ando place in history. Thereby they can dispense with any essentialist notions about permanent and universal social statuses; the floating context that affects human meaning-making is also illustrated.

A third value and purpose of the exercise lies in instigating change in students' relationships to their cultures. In this third step they identify their relationship to their culture, or their "cultural identity orientation." If they are "naïve" about one of their cultures, or immersed in it, they are especially challenged to take more responsibility for the ways in which they make meaning through that cultural lens. The instructor challenges them to step back and look at their culture's power over them, so that they can then make more "multicultural" choices. Another term for such relative "liberation" from a culture is "critical consciousness" (Freire, 1994).

The activity serves a final, more concrete function: As students identify their associations with the various cultural groups, they get to know one another. They come to value the unique contributions of each class member. Thus, this activity is suited to the first class session of any course. However, it serves best as the introductory session for a course in "social and cultural issues," because it foreshadows much of the work of that course.

Objectives

- to introduce the notion of social construction to students

- to instigate recognition of status and power differences among cultural groups

- to have students identify their current cultural group associations

- to broaden the definition of "culture" from the typical ethnicity and race notions to at least eight categories

- to introduce students to each other

Description of the Activity

Phase One. This introductory exercise occurs in four phases, beginning with private reflections and moving on to class discussions. First, students receive the "Cultural Group Memberships Worksheet" (see Appendix). They privately name the cultural groups that they belong to, across eight categories. The eight categories can be remembered by the acronym, "GARREACS," whose letters stand for gender, ability/disability, race, religion, ethnicity, age, class, and sexual orientation. Students then share their cultural group affiliations. During the naming process and the sharing of the varying names for each category, the class begins to note the social construction of the very cultural groups themselves. For example, the blending of ethnicity and race in certain groups (for example, "African-American," or "Jamaican-American," and "Black") generally causes some confusion as students try to understand their own and others' cultural groups. Further, the usual racial designations—Black, Hispanic, Asian, White-non Hispanic—begin to be questioned, as students recognize how limiting they are. For instance, they ask questions such as: How did we decide to group people from Brazil, Mexico, and Spain together under one category? How might those from the Middle East be designated? What do we lose or gain by grouping people from such varying countries as China, Japan, Thailand, and India together as "Asian Americans?" Students may begin to see the categories as fluid, that is, as contingent upon their time and place in history. Students can later discuss their currently preferred terms for their and other groups, and the reasons for such.

Phase Two. The second phase of the activity asks students to identify the broadly understood status or power of their groups in American (or other) society. They must decide on whether their groups are "dominant" or "non-dominant" in most contexts. Students first privately indicate "dominant" or "non-dominant" on the worksheet. Then, the instructor asks students to stand up, first if they are in the dominant gender group, then if they are in the dominant ability-disability group. Standing up or sitting down, that is, being higher than or lower than others, simulates power relationships in society, and simultaneously can trigger an affective experience of being powerful or lacking power. Further, being forced to identify one's power or status position can lead to discussions of context – that is, how various settings impact students' experiences of status and power and how statuses of groups shift as settings, time, and social attitudes change.

Phase Three. Students next review the five "Cultural Group Orientations" (CGO's) See Appendix, column three) and decide on their general awareness of and relationship to each of the eight cultural groups. This phase allows students to note their "naivete" about, or their relative awareness of, cultural influences. For dominant group members, this part of the exercise can be a "wake-up call." They have often taken for granted the dominance of their cultural group, are blind to their cultural assumptions, and have been able to afford to ignore the experiences of minority individuals. For the non-dominant groups, it can be a signal to "get over" their sense of inferiority or their acceptance of prescribed roles.

Phase Four. Following the private writing in each of the three initial phases, students may be divided into groups of four or five to introduce their "cultural selves" and to discuss what stood out when they did the activities. They might be asked to bring back any sources of confusion or disagreement to the larger group.

By the time students reassemble in the large group, they have "broken the ice" with each other, and they have been introduced to three of the overarching concepts of a course in Social and Cultural Issues: (1) cultural group membership; (2) status, power, and hierarchy; and (3) cultural identity developmental level. The instructor asks for reports from each group and notes themes and controversies on the board. She or he can then ask students why such notions might be important to their future counseling work.

Students have now been experientially introduced to the constructs that will be presented during the semester (or during the program, if this activity is done in a course other than Social and Cultural Issues). They also have a beginning awareness of the fluidity and social constructedness of the central notions to be presented during the course or during the counseling program; any dangerous "essentialisms" about culture have begun to be challenged.

REFERENCES

Belenky, M., Clinchy, B., Goldberger, N., & Tarule, J. (1986*). Women's ways of knowing*. New York: Basic Books.

Freire, P. (1994). *Pedagogy of the oppressed*. New York: Continuum.

Kegan, R. (1994). *In over our heads: The mental demands of modern life*. Cambridge: Harvard University Press.

Loevinger, J. (1976). *Ego development: Conceptions and theories*. San Francisco: Jossey-Bass.

McAuliffe, G. J., & Lovell, C. W. (2000). Guidelines for constructivist and developmental instruction. In G. McAuliffe & K. Eriksen. *Preparing counselors and therapists: Creating constructivist and developmental programs*. Alexandria, VA: Association for Counselor Education and Supervision.

Sexton, T.L., & Griffin, B.L. (Eds.). (1997). *Constructivist thinking in counseling practice, research, and training* (pp. 211-227). New York: Teachers College.

APPENDIX

Identifying Your Own Cultural Groups

(Adapted from the Social Justice Education Program, University of Massachusetts at Amherst)

Below are ten categories of cultural groups. As you read each of the groups on the left,

1. Name your own group in the second column. Use whatever label makes sense currently to you. (Note: You may be asked to share as many of these as you are comfortable with.)

2. Then note in the next column whether you see each of your groups as "dominant" (for example, generally in a position of greater power and/ or favor at the current time and place) or "subordinate" (a group whose access to social power is generally limited or denied).

3. Read over the "Five Social Identity Orientations" Model (see descriptions below) and note your current general cultural awareness in column four.

Cultural Identity Category	Your Own Group (Label)	Whether Your Group is Generally Dominant or Subordinate	Your Current Level of Cultural Awareness* (1-5)
Gender			
Ability			
Race			
Religion			
Ethnicity			
Age			
Class			
Sexual Orientation			

*Levels of Cultural Awareness: 1=naïve/acceptant; 2=encountering; 3=immersed; 4=reflective; 5=multicultural.

FIVE ORIENTATIONS TOWARD YOUR CULTURAL GROUP MEMBERSHIP(S): INTEGRATED MODEL

(Adapted by Garrett McAuliffe, Old Dominion University, from the racial and cultural theories of Helms; Ivey; and D'Andrea and Daniels)

NOTE: These orientations can be applied to any cultural group membership, whether it be gender, age, race, religion, ethnicity, ability/disability, social class, and sexual orientation.

1. NAME THE RELEVANT CULTURAL GROUP:_____

2. NAME THE ORIENTATION BELOW THAT BEST CHARACTERIZES YOUR CURRENT AWARENESS FOR THIS GROUP MEMBERSHIP: _____

Orientation One: Naïve/Acceptant
Unaware of own cultural situatedness; unaware of power differentials among social groups ("What do you mean, 'What are the assumptions of my cultural group?' I'm just a human, like everyone else! We're all the same. I don't think about it. I'm just me."

Orientation Two: Encountering
Beginning awareness that personal history can affect one's assumptions and beliefs. Unaware of power and oppression in society (My family is very authoritarian; that's why I am.").

Orientation Three: Immersed
Discovery of one's social identity. Immersion in cultural activities, reading about the culture, celebration of the group's fight against social inequity, infused with cultural styles, music, customs. (I now realize how many assumptions I've made about being a woman that limit me."). Often mystification about or denigration of other groups (Intolerant version: "I don't understand why they have to talk so loudly. We always keep conversations private." or "I can't believe that they put earrings in children's ears! How weird!")

Orientation Four: Reflective
Can stand back from personal and cultural history; can choose cultural attributes that one wishes to claim, reclaim, or discard. Can see patterns of oppression between groups. Recognizes the constructed "story" of one's cultural group.

Orientation Five: Multicultural
Committed to universal care and rights. Dedicated to amelioration of oppressive conditions. Can take multiple perspectives, is empathic and compassionate. Recognizes effects of oppression on all groups. Can see dilemmas even for dominant group. Interested in instigating dialogue.

MINDING OUR MANNERS: AN ACTIVITY
FOR CONSTRUCTING ETHNICITY
—Garrett McAuliffe

A primary, and preliminary, task for diversity-sensitive counselors is to become aware of their own cultures. Such awareness is the first of the three major multicultural counseling competencies (Sue, Arredondo, & McDavis, 1992). Without personal cultural awareness, a counselor is liable to project her own manners and worldview onto the client. From this ethnocentric frame, a counselor may pathologize what is for that client culturally appropriate in the situation, or conversely, may normalize what should be considered problematic. For instance, the Irish-American counselor who has not re-examined her cultural heritage might minimize attention to behaviors clearly indicating alcohol abuse, while a Muslim counselor might over-pathologize any alcohol use.

One facet of cultural awareness is understanding of one's own ethnicity. Ethnicity often carries with it tacit assumptions about what is good, beautiful, and true. Ethnicity-based socialization influences our views, from what is worth striving for to what is mannerly or rude. Ethnicity-based assumptions frequently lurk underneath our conscious awareness, powerfully influencing our sense of shame or guilt, our gender roles, our allegiances to communality or individualism, and our notions of beauty, and our allegiances. For example, the high-involvement, expressive Italian dinner table might look chaotic and unmannerly to the Anglo-American whose sense of propriety requires longer pauses in conversation and more moderation in tone of voice. Yet despite its unmistakable role in human life and behavior, in Giordano and Carini-Giordano's words "Ethnicity is a powerful, but little-understood concept in therapy" (1997, p.1).

It is beyond the purpose of this segment to probe the complexities of ethnicity or its psychological and counseling implications. The reader is referred to the work of Jean Phinney (1996) for further exploration of such. Let it suffice here to remind ourselves that ethnicity is a slippery concept, and we need to qualify any generalizations we draw about it. The salience of ethnicity varies from person to person: multi-ethnicity abounds, race is often conflated with ethnicity, social class and religion mix in and thus influence the expression of ethnicity. Finally, recency of immigration and minority status play major roles in one's ethnic experience (Phinney, 1996). It is safe to say, however, that every human being is "ethnic," whether she knows it or not. And those who do not know it play a dangerous game, for their worldview becomes mistaken for the universal definition of "the good." If she has power, that view can be imposed on others, with disastrous consequences for clients or even for whole populations.

The following activity seeks to counter those dangers by increasing counselors' awareness of their ethnicity. "Minding our Manners" asks future counselors to assess their current ideas about their ethnicity, to determine the salience of what might be their various ethnicities, and to evaluate what aspects of ethnicity they would keep and what aspects they would like to eschew. In this activity, students engage in the seemingly contradictory activities of first knowing and naming their ethnic identity and its accompanying assumptions, only to then deconstruct, and/or affirm, or perhaps distance themselves from such assumptions. Thus emerges the tension of becoming multicultural: Knowing and holding one's cultural identities, while at the same time "taking them as object" (Kegan, 1982) and relativizing them in a constant process of deconstruction. The activity ends with the possibility of re-naming, of becoming "less ethnic," or less ethnocentric, and more multicultural.

This activity thus starts at the beginning, by asking students to respond to the question, "Who are my people?" "What have I learned from them?" "How have they adapted to life?" After naming both his or her ethnicity and its assumptions, the student must then decide on the salience, or importance, of that ethnic identity for her. For instance, ethnicity has been found to be more salient for members of minority groups and recent immigrants (Phinney, 1996), while members of the dominant ethnic group commonly treat their worldview and customs as "normal," "regular," or, worse, as "reality." All other ethnicities, to some, are variations on the "real" theme of being a "White American." Such a Cultural identity and set of assumptions that remain unspoken may be essentialized, that is, considered to be the "normal," or, "what everyone would be or is trying to be." As one of my students discovered, many of her ideas about what she had thought was "appropriate" had been formed by her "aristocratic, class conscious, Anglo, White, Episcopalian Virginian grandparents," whose ancestors had had a plantation in horse country and to whom she had been sent for training in proper manners. I would propose that awareness of these "forgotten" customs and habits should remain salient for the counselor who is poised to help clients reconstruct their own experiences. We need to do first what we would expect of others, I would propose.

In the process of naming and stepping back from ethnic assumptions, a student can be drawn into the world of social construction, that is, a world in which ethnic labels and assumptions are recognized as the creations of a community with a common heritage, and that they are no more "real" than those created by other communities. I have designed the following activity to illuminate these notions. The activity is both developmental and constructivist: It invites a student to move from a habitual, conformist worldview to one in which construction is recognized as pervasive.

Objectives

- To name one's own ethnicity or ethnicities.

- To know the general characteristics of these groups.

- To determine how those characteristics affect one's current life.

- To decide on the salience of these ethnicities for oneself.

- To learn about the characteristics of other ethnic groups and the implications of these for counseling.

Description of the Activity

The research and the writing. Students first do out-of-class research on the social and psychological characteristics of their ethnic group(s). They begin with personal exploration, responding to questions that evoke family and ethnic assumptions and customs. Questions, such as: How did your family express negative and/or positive emotions? Affection? How did they "do" conflict? What gender roles were practiced? What customs did you observe? What ethnic culture might they represent? What groups and practices were considered undesirable?

Students then move to the broader domain of general ethnic characteristics by reading about their own ethnic group(s) in McGoldrick, Pearce, and Giordano's *Ethnicity and Family Therapy* (1996). They also consult one other written source on their ethnic group. Additionally, they are encouraged to interview a family member. These inquiries culminate in a five-to-six page paper called "My Ethnic Identity: A Personal Exploration."

In-class peer instruction. On the day that the paper is due, students gather in groups to share their research on ethnic characteristics and to explore counseling implications. Two alternatives are possible here:

1). *Single Ethnicity Groups.* Students mill around and find members of their own ethnic group. Then they retire to a separate space and discuss the following:

- What was it like to find your group just now? How did you locate them and how did you decide what to call your group? (The social construction of group labels is thereby evoked).

   – Decide what you will call yourselves.

– What feelings do you have about being part of this group: pride? solidarity? discomfort? embarrassment?

– Discuss the common characteristics of "your people." Write down key points on poster paper.

– Name important issues a counselor might alert herself to if she were to work with members of your group. List those on the poster paper.

– (Optional) Prepare a role play that might demonstrate some helpful ideas for working with a member of your group.

– Name the limits of these generalizations. Where are stereotypes possible? How do these generalizations fit your own experience? How salient is ethnicity to each of you?

– On the basis of their discussions together, students plan a short presentation entitled "Important Issues in Working with _____ (name of ethnic group)," that highlights both the differences and universalities among members of their group.

2. *Multi-ethnic groups.* Students are mixed in small groups composed of four or five people of different ethnicities. In these multi-ethnic groups, each student shares her ethnic group's characteristics. Students also note the commonalities among ethnic groups. They prepare a presentation that again highlights both the key characteristics of each of their groups and the common elements among groups.

Each method of small group sharing has advantages and disadvantages. In the first, the recognition and discovery of common, shared experiences allows the group to bring a coherent presentation to the rest of the class. However, this method of presentation highlights differences rather than the far greater commonalities shared by all human groups. The second option focuses more on those universals, but the differences cause the group presentation to be less focused.

Large-group presentation and discussion. The next phase of the activity has the small groups display their posters and present key notions from the questions. After the presentations, the instructor leads a whole group discussion on salience, stereotypes, the role of family in carrying ethnicity, variations due to acculturation, temperament, region, and the influence of religion and social class on ethnicity.

CONCLUSION

Profound discoveries emerge during this activity. Some students begin to discover the broad notion of social construction through recognition of their ethnicity. Many experience affirmation and solidarity, a connection to "their people." I worry with them about the essentialist fallacy: That ethnicity is somehow an entity, not a fluid, context-based construction. We discuss tribalism, that descent into faction and feud that has characterized so much of human history. We reassert the commonalities that we all share, universals like aspiration, fear, procreation, loneliness, support, and survival. Finally, we acknowledge the great variation among individuals in an ethnic group, differences that are far greater within groups than between groups. In the end, we are no longer strangers to ourselves or others.

REFERENCES

Giordano, J., & Carini-Giordano, M. (1995). Ethnicity: The hidden dimension in family counseling/therapy. *The Family Digest, 10,*1-4.

Kegan, R. (1982). *The evolving self.* Cambridge MA: Harvard University Press.

McGoldrick, M., Pearce, J., & Giordano, J. (Eds.). (1996). *Ethnicity and family therapy.* New York: Guilford.

Phinney, J. S. (1996). When we talk about American ethnic groups, what do we mean? *American Psychologist, 51,* 918-927.

Sue, D. W., Arredondo, P., & McDavis, R. J. (1992). Multicultural counseling competencies and standards: A call to the profession. *Journal of Multicultural Counseling and Development, 20,* 64-88.

PARTICIPATORY ACTIVITIES FOR DIVERSITY TRAINING

—*Marilyn J. Montgomery, Raquel Contreras,*
Aretha Faye Marbley, William M. Kurtines

Our many years of collective experience in working with multicultural and ethnically diverse counselors-to-be have been both difficult and rewarding. They have been challenging, and often frustrating, because they have confirmed for us the validity of the claim that our profession has, knowingly or unknowingly, engaged in a form of marginalization. This marginalization has two distressing tendencies: first, the exclusion of non-majority people from participating in counseling as clients (Sue & Sue, 1977, 1990); second, the low participation of non-majority people as professionals and colleagues (D'Andrea & Daniels, 1995).

We have also found our experiences challenging because of a particular paradox that frequently emerges in efforts to implement diversity training, namely, the paradox of "requiring" sensitivity to diversity. We, like others (Steward, Morales, Bartell, Miller, & Weeks, 1998), have often found students resistant to diversity "training" when they sense that facilitators who ostensibly teach the valuing of diversity insist that everyone adopt a particular value, even a "multicultural" value. In our work, we have found that both majority and minority students often find this aspect of the multicultural "canon" to be narrow and limiting.

Our experiences, nevertheless, have been rewarding because we have also become convinced of the importance to our profession of responding actively to the issue of inclusion (Fouad, 1999; Sue, Arredondo, & McDavis, 1992). To be truly inclusive, we must create approaches that welcome *all* marginalized and under-represented trainees, including those who have alternative (from ours) conceptions of the work they wish to do. We must continue to find ways to recognize the diversity of human experience in our students and to include their *many* voices in the professional dialogue.

Here we share with you some participatory learning activities that we find to represent a "nonoppressive" approach to diversity training. These activities grew out of our efforts to develop a theoretically grounded approach using participatory learning and transformative activities with both majority and non-majority trainees. In our work, we came to realize that in order to promote the value of inclusiveness we must genuinely listen to *all* of our students. Through our interactions with them, we began to wonder: Who should determine the diversity training curriculum? If the instructor determines the curriculum and sets forth the competencies that will be achieved, is this an implicitly "oppressive method"? If so, what could we do to ensure that in our own classrooms, the "local and particular" voice was heard?

To fully address this issue, we developed approaches in which our students were active co-participants in the creation of the learning context and process. We found that the use of participatory learning process helped to resolve the paradox of "requiring" that students adopt a particular multicultural agenda because it offers a model of teaching and learning that is collaborative rather than didactic. Participatory learning is also more consistent with the establishment of collaborative counseling relationships—the kind we find most empowering for clients (Steward, 1998). Rather than using an approach that dictates an endpoint, participatory learning processes directly involve students in determining what is to be included in the training curriculum.

We believe this is the best approach for transforming our profession into one that is truly inclusive. To this end, we have adopted the "transformative pedagogy" of Paulo Freire (1970/1983). Our goal with minority trainees in doing so has been to open them to the possibility of transforming (rather than enduring) the circumstances that negatively impact their personal and professional lives and the life of their communities. Our goal with majority trainees has been to open them to the possibility of taking social action to reduce the injustices that continue to exist in contemporary social forms. We hope such a pedagogy allows *all* students to acquire a greater critical understanding of themselves (as racial, cultural persons) and of the contexts (of privilege or marginalization, or both) in which they live. We see this as a step toward liberating our individual students, ourselves, and our profession from both subtle and overt forms of oppression (Ivey, 1995).

The Participatory Learning Activities

In contrast to training approaches relying on directive and didactic processes, participatory learning experiences emphasize cooperative and mutual learning contexts. Mutual sharing of knowledge and reciprocal learning takes place between the students and the teacher. For example, from the instructor, the students can learn about diversity-sensitizing concepts for the delivery of counseling services. From the students, the instructor can learn what life has taught them about the practical and political issues of getting along and getting ahead in their own cultural settings.

Processes and Objectives

We use *exploration* and *problem posing* to accomplish training goals. The class group becomes a starting point from which both students and the teacher *explore* their own cultural competence. As the group becomes more cohesive and inclusive, members challenge one another to think critically about:

- their awareness and sensitivity to diversity,

- the assumptions, motivations, and cultural agendas they bring to the counseling context,

- their level of knowledge about cultural issues that are "local and particular" (migrant issues, immigration issues, local ethnic politics),

- their level of general cultural skills, local and particular cultural skills, and competencies for dealing with clients.

The next section will describe five participatory learning activities that we have found helpful in achieving these goals. These activities are intended to encourage each student to actively participate. In conducting the activities, we have found that the members of the group support one another as they gather information, encounter resistance, uncover surprising (both distressing or encouraging) facts, and draw new conclusions. Some students are comfortable with all activities; others become quite anxious (and less able to profit from the experience in a constructive way) with some activities. Offering opportunities for choices in participation, however, allows students to choose their optimal level of challenge.

The organization and structure of the activities draw on the type of group exercise activities commonly used in diversity training, but we have adapted them to fit the participatory goals of our training program. We describe the activities in the sequence that we have found useful, but the selection (number, type, content, etc.) of the activities can be adapted for particular contexts. The first two activities focus on enhancing cultural *awareness*, the third focuses on enhancing *knowledge* of particular groups, and the last two activities increase students' diversity *skills*, particularly their perspective-taking and role-taking skills.

AWARENESS OF ONE'S OWN CULTURE

In this activity, students explore and discover the roots of their own cultural values and share information about their cultural tradition with others in the group. Many students experience this activity as extremely meaningful, and many have been very creative with their sharing. One person, for example, brought a poster with her "life in pictures," from baby pictures until the present. Another person brought a special type of bread that had special memories from childhood. This person served the bread to each participant, as it was her cultural tradition for women to serve meals.

Another person brought very old albums of music that had special relevance to her culture. Yet another person brought a handout with a brief description of her religion and used her time to explain how her faith shaped her values.

Instructions to participants. We say, "This experience is intended to raise awareness about your own culture by encouraging you to discover your cultural values. In the process of gathering factual information about yourself, you may arrive at insights that are emotionally laden. Feel free to share only what is within your level of comfort. Because this information about your cultural tradition will be shared with others, it also provides them with the opportunity to get to know you in ways that may be emotionally laden. Again, feel free to share only what is within your level of comfort."

Facilitator instructions. This time-intensive activity will need to be completed at a time other than class time. It is recommended that several three-hour lab times be set up by the instructor to accommodate the entire class in groups of six.

- Have students sign up for the three-hour lab time, preferably with six other people they do not know.

- Define "culture" as Smith and Vasquez (1985) do: "shared values, shared perceptions of reality, and shared symbols that people have by which their thinking and interpersonal relationships are conducted" (p. 532).

- Have students identify components of their culture before coming to the lab. The following questions may facilitate self-exploration:

Identify attributes that characterize you.

How did these attributes emerge? Who in your family has them? Who doesn't?

What are some of your family traditions? Holidays? Foods? Music? Occupations? Religious practices? Jewelry?

Identify your family tree as far back as you can go. To what geographic regions can you trace your ancestors? This information may be available from parents and elder relatives.

- Have students select what cultural material they are willing to share with their group of six. This material must be able to be presented in 20 minutes per participant.

Instructions for the 3-hour lab

1. Have the eight students sit in a circle. Reintroduce the information given in the Instructions to Participants.

2. Allow students to select the sharing order and allow each student no more than 20 minutes. (6 students x 20 minutes each = 120 minutes, out of 180 minutes total)

Suggestions for facilitation of the sharing

1. Set up the expectation that there is no "right or wrong" way of sharing. Each student is the expert in his/her own cultural experience.

2. Set up an atmosphere of acceptance of the uniqueness of each individual presenting.

3. At times, a presenter may experience strong emotions. Validate that experience.

Affective processing. Utilize the last 20 minutes of the 3-hour period for affective processing. This component can also be expanded to include a written/homework portion in which students can select one or several questions and write a brief essay on them.

1. What led to your volunteering to share your culture at the time that you did?

2. What went into your selection of the components of your culture that you shared?

3. Any reactions to fellow students? What piece of other student's culture touched you?

4. What was it like to define your culture in this manner?

5. What was it like for you to share information about your culture with others?

6. How did you feel before the sharing? How do you feel now?

7. What did you learn about yourself?

8. How can you use this self-knowledge to understand others?

AWARENESS OF DIFFERENCES

This activity raises consciousness about differences. Students select one form of diversity, develop an operational definition, and define anchors along the continuum for this form of diversity. We recommend starting with less emotionally laden forms of diversity such as birth order (oldest, youngest, middle), residential background (urban, suburban, rural), or gender. We recommend that emotionally laden forms of diversity such as ethnicity or sexual orientation not be explored until the class has reached a high level of acceptance of diversity and until the instructor is willing to process individual reactions, even outside of class.

Instructions to participants. We say, "This activity is intended to raise consciousness about differences. By definition, change, even positive change, is stressful, and increasing your awareness about differences is a form of change. Feel free to discontinue this activity at any time by walking, quietly, away from the small group."

Facilitator instructions

- For this exercise, the class participates as a group.

- Select one form of diversity, develop an operational definition and define anchors along the continuum of this form of diversity. For example, birth order (oldest, youngest, middle), residential background (urban, rural), gender. Again we recommend that the most emotionally laden forms of diversity, such as ethnicity or sexual orientation, not be utilized until the class has reached a high level of acceptance of diversity and the instructor is willing to process individual reactions, even outside of class.

- Involve the class in developing descriptors for each anchor and write them on the board.

As each anchor is read, have the students raise their right hand if they belong to the group defined by the anchor, for example, oldest child.

As each descriptor under the defined anchor is read, have the students who belong to that particular group stand up if the descriptor applies to them.

- Provide an example. One neutral continuum of diversity that we often start with is diversity of clothing on a cold day—Wearing a coat, vs. sweater, vs. neither. The objective is to place people into meaningful categories that are not shame-based or painfully prejudicial so that people can come to accept diversity as a way of life. Since the "benign" forms of diversity proposed by the activity are typically not painful, or even subject to change, people can become comfortable with displaying and discussing diversity. We like to close the activity by introducing the idea that, in contrast to the forms of diversity used in the exercise, other forms of diversity are defined pejoratively, to some extent, by forces outside the individual. These pejorative evaluations can limit the individual possesses the devalued characteristics.

Affective processing. Include the entire class in the discussion as class members share their emotional reactions. Suggested questions for discussion might include:

1. What was it like to identify your belonging to the defined anchor?

2. What was your reaction as you stood up to show identification with each descriptor under the anchors?

3. What did you learn about yourself?

INCREASING YOUR KNOWLEDGE ABOUT LOCAL AND PARTICULAR ETHNIC GROUPS

This activity increases students' *knowledge* about the ethnic groups of class members. Rather than focusing on the content of every group's culture, this activity provides the opportunity for the students to share in the experience of being a member of particular non-majority ethnic groups. Although we present this as a single exercise, it can be repeated for as many ethnic groups as are locally relevant. It can also be broadened to include other types of cultural or lifestyle diversity.

Instructions to participants. "This is an imagery activity intended to increase your knowledge about [ethnic group]. The focus is not on the content of this group's culture, but on the experience of what it is like to be a member of a non-majority ethnic group. Participation is strictly voluntary and you may choose not to participate or to withdraw from participation at any time during the exercise. If you choose not to participate or to withdraw from participation, please remain quiet and respectful of the students who are participating."

Facilitator instructions. This activity requires students to be more vulnerable. We recommend that it be done after the class group has developed a sense of cohesion and members feel some level of comfort with the instructor and with each other.

- Prior to the lectures:

  For a given ethnic group, generate, through class discussion, stereotypes or descriptors of the ethnic group. For example, ask, "When you hear the term "African American" what comes to your mind?" Write these on the board without discussion or judgment. Next, lead the students through the following imagery exercise:

  Take a deep breath. Inhale, hold it, exhale . . . . One more deep breath, full air intake. . . exhale. . . . One more time . . . inhale . . . exhale. (The idea is to focus the student's attention on the breathing. Guide the students' attention through the breathing cycle—typically 3-7 times.) You may close your eyes, if you like, in order to follow my imagery.

  For this exercise of 10 minutes, I would like of you to imagine being [ethnic group in question; for example, African American]. You are a student at [name of University] and on this [day, month, year] you are sitting at your desk for [class]. You became keenly aware that your ethnicity is different from the majority of the class's ethnicity.
  You got up this morning, got yourself dressed and ready for school just like you do every school day. (The idea is to anchor the experience in real aspects of their experience.)
  Today was similar to all your other mornings in many ways. One big difference for today is that you are [ethnic group].

  For the next portion of the imagery exercise, weave in general, factual elements about the ethnic group. In addition, introduce the descriptors generated by the class, prefaced by "Some people believe that . . . . Some people are of the opinion . . . . Some people have arrived to the conclusion . . . . " (It is very important to introduce the descriptors generated by the class in a non-judgmental way and as the opinion of "some people."). At the end of the activity, say, "Let me bring your attention to your breathing once again. Take a deep breath . . . . " (Repeat as necessary.) "You may open your eyes gently. Take your time . . . ."

Process the imagery experience. Give the class the option not to answer these questions out loud, but just to ponder each question in their quest for deeper understanding and knowledge of others.

1. For those of you who participated, how did you arrive at this decision? Likewise, the ones who chose not to participate?

2. What was it like to take the ethnic identity of [ethnic group] for ten minutes?

3. How well could you let go of your own ethnicity and become [ethnic group]?

4. When you became [ethnic group], what was it like for you to hear the opinions, beliefs, and conclusions drawn by some people?

5. Knowing your opinion of [ethnic group] before the exercise, has this opinion been altered after the exercise? If yes, how?

*   Becoming informed

    Present a lecture with information on a group [ethnic] , to include the history, current demographic trends, traditions, world-view.

    Write on the board the stereotypes and descriptors [of the ethnic group] generated previously. Facilitate discussion to alter these descriptors if the class so desires. Again, accept descriptors in a non-judgmental manner. Repeat the imagery exercise.

    Process the imagery. As shown previously, the benefit from this activity may come in the form of the students' willingness to ask themselves the questions even if they choose not to share the answers with the class.

1. For those of you who participated, how did you arrive at this decision? Likewise, the ones who chose not to participate? Did some of you participate one time and not the other? Both times? Neither time?

2. What was it like to take the ethnic identity of [ethnic group] for ten minutes for a second time?

3. How was this time different from last time? How the same?

4. This time, what was it like to become [ethnic group], what was it like for you to hear the opinions, beliefs, and conclusions drawn by some people?

5. What opinions do you hold about [ethnic group] now?

ASSUMING ANOTHER'S ETHNIC IDENTITY
THROUGHOUT ROLE-TAKING

Perspective-taking skills are essential to the helping professions. These activities sharpen their use in multicultural counseling contexts. Role taking and role playing exercises offer opportunities for people to assume the perspectives of others. They offer methods for further developing skills for interacting with individuals who live in and experience different modes of being in the world. For this activity, we adapt the role-play to focus on the "ethnic identity" of the another.

Students divide into dyads with someone they don't know well who is of a different ethnic identity. Each pair takes turns sharing information about themselves (within the limits of comfort) with their partner. The students finish the activity by taking the ethnic identity of their partner while self-disclosing to the group. This activity may be broadened to include other kinds of cultural or lifestyle diversity.

Facilitator instructions

• Ask for six volunteers and have these six students arrange their desks in a circle in the middle of the room.

• Have students divide into dyads with someone they don't know who is of a different ethnic identity. Define the role of one as "Talker" and the other as "Listener."

Have "Talker" speak to "Listener" for five minutes, sharing information about self (within the limits of comfort) as a member of that ethnic group.

Reverse roles and do the same.

• Ask each of the six students to "take the ethnic identity" of their partner while self-disclosing to the rest of the group. Have the person who is speaking, stand in the middle of the circle. Use first person expressions.

Affective processing. Include the entire class in the discussion as each class member shares his or her emotional reactions. Suggested questions for discussion might include:

1. For the six volunteers, what led to your volunteering? What is the reaction to the activity by the students who did not volunteer?

2. What was it like to sit in the circle in the middle of the room?

3. For the students outside the circle, what did you do for the ten minutes that the students in the circle were talking?

4. For the volunteers, what was it like to speak about yourself for five minutes? What was it like for someone to listen to you for five minutes?

5. What was it like to take the identity of someone else in front of the class?

6. What would it be like to live from the perspective of your partner for an entire day? week? month?

7. What did you learn about yourself?

EXPERIENCING ANOTHER'S ETHNIC IDENTITY THROUGH THE EXPRESSIVE ARTS

This activity uses role taking and role playing exercises that are rooted in the expressive arts. The expressive arts offer a ready-made opportunity for people to empathically "step into other people's shoes." Novels and films offer verbal and visual vehicles for experiencing the world of others; they are intentionally created to be powerful and influential experiences. In this exercise, small groups present a novel or film to the rest of the students through dramatic readings or enactments of particularly poignant portions of the novel or films. The group then discusses these renditions.

Facilitator instructions

*   Ask the class members to individually compile a list of books or films that they believe capture important elements of the experience of people in their region, both historically and currently. In particular, help them identify books or films that are produced by persons of a particular group, portraying the significant stories of that group. To extend this experience, novel or film characters can be used to practice case conceptualizations that include attention to the broad systemic influences upon the character's past and present.

*   Have class members share the list of books (or films) that they find particularly powerful in offering a locally relevant perspective.

- Have small groups of volunteers read the same novel (or see the same film) to facilitate dialogue about the novel's themes and characters.

    Small groups can be asked to present the novel or film to the rest of the students by finding a way to make it "come alive" through dramatic readings or enactments of particularly poignant portions of the novel.

    Groups discuss of these renditions.

    Affective processing. Have entire class share their emotional reactions. Suggested questions for discussion:

1. For the small group volunteers, what led to your volunteering? What is the reaction to the activity by the students who did not volunteer?

2. What was it like to immerse yourself in the dramatic reading?

3. What was it like to portray this in front of the class?

4. For the students watching the enactment, what did you feel during the enactment?

5. What would it be like to live in the role of your character for an entire day? Week? Month?

6. What did you learn about yourself?

REFERENCES

D'Andrea, M., & Daniels, J. (1995). Promoting multiculturalism and organizational change in the counseling profession. In J. Ponterotto, J. M. Casas, L. A. Suzuki, & C. M. Alexander (Eds.), *Handbook of multicultural counseling,* (pp. 17-33), Thousand Oaks: Sage.

Fouad, N. A. (1999). Diversity and the public interest. *Division 17 Newsletter (American Psychological Association, Division of Counseling Psychology), 20* (2), 3-5.

Freire, P. (1970/1983). *Pedagogy of the oppressed.* New York: Continuum.

Ivey, A. E. (1995). Psychotherapy as liberation. In Ponterotto, J. G., Casas, J. M., Suzuki, L. A., & Alexander, C. M. (Eds.). *Handbook of multicultural counseling,* (pp. 53-72). Thousand Oaks: Sage.

Smith, E. M. J., & Vasquez, M. J. T. (Eds.). (1985). Cross-cultural counseling. *The Counseling Psychologist, 13,* 531-684.

Steward, R. J. (1998, April). PAR: A theoretic model for self-assessment and practice toward multicultural counseling competence. *In integrating theory, researc, training, and practice toward multicultural competence.* Symposium conducted at the American Counseling Association World Conference, Indianapolis, Indiana.

Steward, R. J., Morales, P. C., Bartell, P. A., Miller, M., & Weeks, D. (1998). The multiculturally responsive versus the multiculturally reactive: A study of perceptions of counselor trainees. *Journal of Multicultural Counseling and Development, 26,* 2-12.

Sue, D. W., Arredondo, P., & McDavis, R. J. (1992). Multicultural counseling competencies and standards: A call to the profession. *Journal of Multicultural Counseling and Development, 20,* 64-88.

Sue, D. W., & Sue, D. (1977). Barriers to effective cross-cultural counseling. *Journal of Counseling Psychotherapy, 24,* 420-429.

Sue, D. W., & Sue, D. (1990). *Counseling the culturally different: Theory and practice,* (2nd ed.). New York: John Wiley.

INTRODUCTION TO CULTURAL ASSIMILATION
—*Karen Eriksen*

It is now an established imperative that we as educators need to develop multicultural awareness, knowledge, and skills, and must assist counseling students to do the same. The following exercise helps students to understand the process of ethnic cultural assimilation by having students ask questions of their own cultural histories and hear about their peers' histories. Studying assimilation reminds students of the varying saliency that ethnicity has for different individuals. It also introduces more assimilated individuals to the continuing influences of their own ethnic culture.

The Introduction to Cultural Assimilation benefits students in other ways as well. Students participate actively in the learning process, which increases retention (Caine & Caine, 1994; McNamara, Scott, Bess, 2000). They bring their own personal histories into the classroom experience, finding the relevance of course material to their personal lives. Further, students hear the voices of their peers and are thus challenged to value the varying perspectives of those around them. The exercise, by its nature, also builds a sense of community and mutual understanding. Finally, it contributes to attitudinal change—that is, to changes in feelings about culture and about people from other cultures—as well as cognitive knowledge.

The students with whom I have done this exercise have seemed surprised that they share common characteristics with others from the same generation of immigrants. Those who have had little exposure to cultural differences or have given little credit to the importance of considering cultural differences become "sold" on the importance of considering cultural differences, even those differences between first and fourth generation immigrants from such European countries as Germany or Denmark. Such an emphasis on generational distance from the "old" country or the reservation helps to avoid the oversimplification of particularism—that is, a focus on a specific ethnicity as a monolithic category that is associated with stereotypical characteristics.

This exercise might be used in a Multicultural Counseling or Counseling Special Populations Course, or in any course which includes a one-class introduction to multicultural issues, such as Introduction to Counseling or Community Counseling.

Objectives

- Introduce students to awareness of their own cultural heritage

- Graphically represent the impact of differing degrees of cultural assimilation

- Increase students' understanding of the experiences of other cultural groups.

Description of the Activity

First students read about and discuss the importance of the counseling process by considering the cultural heritage of both the client and the counselor. Also it would be good if the instructor has already presented theories and definitions of assimilation and acculturation (for instance, Falicov, 1988 or Robinson & Howard-Hamilton, 2000). The instructor now introduces this two-part activity. First, class members turn to a partner to discuss for a few minutes what they understand their cultural heritage to be and how it impacts them today. Partners share with each other answers to such questions as, "What is your ethnic cultural heritage?" "What evidence of your heritage exists in your current family? . . . In your family of origin?" "How does your cultural heritage impact your life today?" "Consider things such as holidays celebrated, holiday traditions, spiritual rituals, language spoken, special foods, and ways in which men and women relate to one another and to children."

Next, the class members divide into groups according to whether they are the first, second, third, or fourth (or more) generation in this country. Generational group members discuss among themselves the impact of their cultural heritage on their current life and then present what they have discovered to the rest of the class. The instructor punctuates each of the discoveries with information from theory or from the assigned readings, and processes the discoveries with the larger group.

REFERENCES

Caine, R.N., & Caine, G. (1994). *Making connections: Teaching and the human brain.* Menlo Park, CA: Addison-Wesley.

Falicov, C. J. (1988). Learning to think culturally. In H. A. Liddle, D. C. Breunlin, & R. C. Schwartz, (Eds.). *Handbook of family therapy training and supervision,* (pp. 334-357), New York: The Guilford Press

McNamara, D. S., Scott, J., & Bess, T. (2000). Building blocks of knowledge: Constructivism from a cognitive perspective. In G. McAuliffe, K. Eriksen, and Associates, *Preparing counselors and therapists: Creating constructivist and developmental programs,* (pp. 62-76). Alexandria, VA: Association for Counselor Education and Supervision.

Robinson, T. & Howard-Hamilton, M. (2000). *The convergence of race, ethnicity, and gender: Multiple identities in counseling.* Columbus, OH: Merrill.

5

Improvisational Activities

Karen Eriksen, Michael O'Connor, and Garrett McAuliffe

"Catharsis," "here and now," "discovery," "interaction," "reflection and revision," "empathy for others' situations," and "vivid recall." These and other descriptors have been used to characterize improvisational teaching and counseling methods. In this chapter, we have joined three specific strategies, that is, dramatic sculpting, role play, gestalt chair work, and simulation, under the rubric of "improvisation." Each of these teaching methods elicits activity, interaction, and collaboration. Each can also generate emotion and discovery. Sometimes these methods trigger tear, embarrassment, and confusion. And they are almost inevitably time-consuming. Under the right conditions, however, the time spent in improvisational activity is worth the effort in retention, empowerment, and cognitive development for students.

The instructor plays three roles in improvisation: facilitator, supporter, and manager. As a "facilitator," the instructor keeps in mind the denotation of the word, "to make easier." She engages in a balancing act of directively and non-directively guiding the experience. She asks students about their experience and makes observations about the process. She ties the experience into course content. The instructor is also a "supporter." Students often find improvisation to be risky, and they need a calm, warm, co-journeyer to stand beside them. "Coaching" might convey the spirit of this support. Finally, the instructor is a "manager" of the activity. Directions should be clear, even written. Time frames and roles need to be spelled out. The manager may need to "referee" if, for example, a student is being criticized in a harsh way.

Improvisation uniquely combines the abstract and the concrete. It allows even the "weakest" students to contribute. So we encourage the use of improvisation in the counselor education classroom from a fervor born of our own experiences of the value of these methods for "discovery learning."

— *Garrett McAuliffe*

DRAMATIC "SCULPTING"
— *Karen Eriksen*

Twenty years ago, while beginning my first internship, I stood on a stage with Virginia Satir as an "actor" who was being "sculpted" into a family system, all because I had the gall to raise my hand and ask for help in understanding a family I was counseling. I was amazed at the depth and color of understanding about the family system that Satir's sculpting of my situation generated for us, as beginning counselors. I was impressed by the clarity with which we were able to "see" how to intervene with the family from this visual and kinesthetic depiction of its dynamics.

Sculpting is a psychodrama-like technique in which participants act out roles at the direction of an instructor, supervisor, or counselor who is seeking help on a case. Sculpting can help both those participating and those watching to understand more clearly how parts of systems—portrayed by the "actors"—engage with and impact one another.

I have incorporated sculpting as a learning strategy into the various forms of supervision that I do—including the practicum and internship classes—because I find sculpting to be so useful in conceptualizing cases and in designing treatment plans. Instructors may also use sculpting when considering cases in courses such as Human Growth and Development, Couples and Family Counseling, Individual Counseling Techniques, Theories of Counseling, and Assessment.

Ssculpting is particularly useful with beginning counselors whose limited understanding of which issues and processes to attend to results in their inability to talk "about" the client, the problem, or the solution in meaningful and colorful ways. Like the use of live data, sculpting assists supervising instructors and students to perceive (using all of their senses) the possibilities for working with particular clients in a more colorful, dramatic, active way.

Sculpting also sends a clear message to students that understanding the client's system is essential to fully understanding the client and to planning interventions. Students broaden their perspectives beyond the traditional views that pathology resides only within the individual when the whole class "acts out" the various factors that place pressure on the clients or oppress them, similarly, sculpting presents dramatically how counselors might be inducted into behavior similar to that of other pressuring or influencing systems. They begin to understand the relative nature of "normal" and "pathological" and to speak in more contextually sensitive and caring language. They examine clients' problems from a larger systems perspective and explore their own roles in contributing to systems that damage individuals.

Sculpting also engages students in the active co-construction of knowledge, which in turn promotes group cohesion and support. Instructors pose questions about possibilities, encouraging student dialogue, interaction, and reflection in considering various hypotheses for case conceptualization and intervention strategies. The instructor's experience allows him or her to pose a wider range of possibilities than students might generate on their own. The "downside" for instructors might seem to lie in their giving up the expert, knowledge-transferring role. Instead they invite students to consider multiple perspectives and to voice their own perspectives, an approach which has been demonstrated to enhance student development (Kegan, 1982; 1994). Such development is related to becoming a more autonomous, thoughtful professional. But it isn't always as comfortable for instructor.

Sculpting promotes cognitive development in at least two ways. As already mentioned, it encourages students to discover and voice their own perspectives, a "challenge" necessary for movement to Kegan's "self-authoring" stage (Kegan, 1982; 1994). Students also find "support" when instructors balance the challenge with clear instructions, directiveness, and structuring of the exercise. Sculpting seems adaptable to both more and less complex students whom. I used sculpting in an internship course with students I had tested with the Learning Environments Preferences Scale (LEP; Moore, 1987). Dualists, multiplists, and relativists (Perry, 1970) all apparently experienced what they voiced in class as "aha's." Also, they reported in their journals that they had incorporated case conceptualizations and interventions from the sculpting into their work with particular clients.

A second way in which sculpting enhances development lies in its encouragement of multiple levels of experiencing. Knowledge can be said to exist on cognitive, emotional, and sensory levels. Students might gain understanding from all of these sources by (1) physically (kinesthetically) acting out their understanding of the client and the client's system and moving their bodies into positions representing their understanding; (2) feeling (emotionally) the client experiences during the drama; (3) seeing (visually) the way in which client systems interact; and, (4) reflecting (cognitively) on the meaning for the case of each type of experience. Using sculpting thus communicates to students the importance of trusting various internal sources of knowing, rather than only trusting information from external authorities.

Students may initially be reluctant to participate in sculpting, not anticipating the helpfulness of this learning mode. However, after experiencing sculpting, students often report that it was the most helpful part of the class. One student reported at the end of the course, "Even though I might not do sculpting out in the field, I find myself more fully visualizing key elements impacting my clients as a result of having sculpted in class." Another student, who tended to be a "subjective" knower (Belenky, Clinchy, Goldberger, Tarule, 1986), was able to create the sculpture and know what to do with the client, even without being able to verbally and systematically articulate her understanding of the case. A student from Kenya, who had difficulty with the English language, and thus difficulty communicating information about his case, became aware that he was doing the same unhelpful things with the client that the other people in the client's life were doing. He had this "aha" moment without receiving criticism from others in the class and without having to manage the English language more adeptly than he could.

Sculpting usually employs 5-10 students. Chairs may be used to represent system members in situations requiring more "actors" than there are class members (I watched Virginia Satir use chairs to represent around 50 participants in one sculpture). Forty-five minutes to an hour per case is often needed when sculpting a client's system.

The Objectives of Sculpting

- To create a visual and kinesthetic representation of clients' problems, taking into consideration or clients' relationships and contexts.

- To to create a visual and kinesthetic representation of the client(s)-counselor relationship, particularly when the counselor is feeling stuck.

- To enable counselors-in-training to develop a clearer understanding of the problem (case conceptualization) and of helpful interventions.

Description of the Activity

Phase One: Initial Sculpture. When a student presents a client, group, couple, or family for supervision, the instructor helps the student to direct class member "actors" in playing the roles of the client, the client's family, and the personification of other components—such as drug addition, illness, financial problems, or racial discrimination—in the client's life system. The student director places each actor around the room in positions that visually represent the role of the system component that he/she is playing. The instructor uses his or her own experience to pose questions about how the actors might be placed. For instance, in sculpting a mother's relationship with her child, the professor might question the student director about several possibilities while physically placing class actors in the respective positions: the over-involved mother with her arms placed around a child in such a way that she seems to smother the child; the detached mother who merely observes her child from a room away; or the helpful mother who offers a hand or a hug when needed.

The professor also poses "social constructionist" questions about what roles race, ethnicity, age, ability levels, gender, sexual identity, religion, and socioeconomic class play in the client's drama and in the students' portrayal of that drama. In that vein, as students represent constructs such as "oppression" in the drama, they generate ideas about how their own lenses or the failure to consider their own lenses may influence their case conceptualizations and interventions.

Phase Two: Discussion. When student directors finish their visual representations of clients and their system, the instructor asks the class, "How would you now articulate the problem presented by the client?" Students then consider ways to articulate the problem from the perspectives of various schools of counseling.

Phase Three: Re-sculpting. A second placement of actors now occurs as the instructor follows this discussion with the question, "What, then, would be your goals and objectives in intervening?" Students answer this question by experimenting with different options. They move the actors into different positions in the drama. During this stage of the exercise, the instructor uses his or her expertise to add to the options being considered and to the observations about the possible consequences of various interventions considered.

Variations and Options. Sculpting may be used to portray clients in their current life contexts or may be used to convey the passage of time. For instance, acting out "snapshots" of the client's system in a stepwise progression through significant developmental events clarifies client needs related to individual or family developmental phases.

Sculpting can also portray the relationship between the counselor and the client or between the counselor and the various components in the client's system. The instructor might ask the counselor to place him or herself in a physical position with the client that symbolically represents how he or she envisions the relationship with that client. Such a representation assists counselors to use themselves in becoming more fully aware of how the client impacts those around her, and of how the client experiences the world. Again, the instructor may pose questions about different ways of relating to the client. For instance, if the client's family seems chaotic, the visual portrayal of the counselor's involvement in the chaos might include the counselor physically "whirling" around in chaos with the family. Class dialogue might help the counselor to discover ways to step out of the chaos. Participating in the drama of chaos might allow the counselor to more fully understand the parallel chaotic experience of the family.

During sculpting, the instructor stimulates active participation from all students by not closing discussions until many possibilities are considered. Students usually find themselves energized and enthusiastic, anxious to contribute their perspectives. By reflecting on all hypotheses generated during "brainstorming" about the system, students find themselves enamored of possibilities generated, and therefore continue to express their perspectives.

REFERENCES

Belenky, M., Clinchy, B., Goldberger, N., & Tarule, J. (1986). *Women's ways of knowing*. New York: Basic Books.

Kegan, R. (1982). *The evolving self*. Cambridge, MA: Harvard University Press.

Kegan, R. (1994). *In over our heads*. Cambridge, MA: Harvard University Press.

Moore, W. S. (1987). *Learning Environment Preferences*. Olympia, WA: Center for the Study of Intellectual Development.

Perry, W. (1970). *Forms of intellectual and ethical development in the college years*. New York: Holt, Rinehart, and Winston.

BEHAVIORAL ROLE PLAY AND GESTALT CHAIR WORK
—Michael O'Connor

Something intrigues me about role-plays, psychodrama, and Gestalt chair work. I could explain this fascination intellectually, supporting it with a number of theoretical rationales (Bandler & Grinder, 1979; Kolb, 1984; Lazarus, 1989; McAuliffe & Lovell, 2000). However, my intrigue is more affective: It is the "fun factor"—the delight we know as teachers when we engage students in a voyage of discovery through experience and reflection. Well-enacted experiential work, followed by meaning making discussion, is not only pedagogically and therapeutically efficacious, it is also engaging for all participants! Engagement and fun can emerge from enactments and simulations, such as the two described in this chapter.

Behavioral role-playing and Gestalt chair work (Corey, 1996A), as I have modified them, are interactive interventions that can stimulate the constructivist impulse in the counselor and can reinvigorate a counseling relationship that has reached a plateau. Likewise, these two strategies, when employed by a constructivist counselor educator, can energize an entire class, a small group, or a supervision dyad by generating reflective hypothesis-building and testing. These activities are suited to Counseling Skills and Counseling Theories courses, and to "lab" courses, such as practicum or internship. I have used them most effectively in small practicum groups (8-10 students) or in individual supervision, although I have also employed them in Counseling Theories classes of 25 in order to demonstrate the application of theory.

Both of these strategies can help instructors who wish to meet Duckworth's (1986, as cited in Sexton and Griffin, 1997, p. 216) two criteria for constructivist teachers: (1) instigating authentic experiences that replicate those phenomena under consideration, and (2) eliciting student thinking about these experiences. Employment of these therapeutic techniques in teaching also fosters student progression through Lovell and McAuliffe's (1997) four epistemologies that are from "authority-constructing" to "dialectical constructing." Students are helped to generate their own ideas and to engage in dialogue about them. And, not to lose sight of another dimension of experiential work, these strategies provide a dose of the "engagement factor," a powerful antidote to boredom and over-abstraction.

In chair work, students report personal benefit from integrating their own polarities. They gain insight into more effective ways of relating to significant individuals in their own lives with whom they have unfinished business. In chair work that continues beyond one or two exchanges, students sometimes gain a visceral experience of the other person or part of self, including the fears, vulnerabilities, and the strengths that influence the other. In addition, by varying the "Dialogue" portion of the work, new ways of coaching the student client are often generated. Students also often brainstorm various ways to foster the "client's" integration of their "opposites."

The most important benefit of these two experiential exercises, from a constructivist standpoint, is the growth that emerges from the synergy of open discourse. Such discourse exemplifies and fosters the co-construction of meanings. This synergistic "multilogue" spawns the phenomenon described by Freire (1971), "Through dialogue, the teacher-of-the-students and the students-of-the-teacher cease to exist and a new term emerges: teacher-student with students-teacher."

Introduction and Objectives

Both of these classroom interventions, which can evoke strong emotions, require adequate relationship building, developing a foundation of trust in the teacher-student relationship. A key component of this relationship building is the open attitude of the instructor. A constructivist approach to teaching is an open approach, fostering a creative, invigorating, mutually-owned process of dialogue-based discovery and meaning-making. This is the orientation of an instructor who knows that, to paraphrase Kierkegaard, (as cited in Kegan, 1994) instruction begins when you place yourself in the [learner's] place so that you may understand what she or he understands in the way that she or he understands it. Also, ample time must be allowed in classes or in counseling sessions for these exercises and for adequate de-briefing in the epilogue. I also tell students that, first and foremost, they must be sensitive to and respectful of limits, and take care in how much they challenge clients during these experiences. The objectives of these activities are:

- To model alternative verbal interventions for students experiencing impasse with their clients.

- To provide students with the opportunity to practice voicing heretofore unspoken thoughts and feelings regarding self or client.

- To assist students to discover and practice alternative interventions for use with clients.

- To provide students and instructors with the opportunity to discover students' tacit assumptions about their clients.

- To provide students with practice in developing alternative perspectives and hypotheses regarding their clients.

- To provide opportunity for teacher-student and student-student dialogue from which to develop new understandings of client-therapist
  issues.

- To introduce students to role-play and Gestalt chair work as experiential interventions through participation on the activity.

Role Reversal Role Play

This activity is a classic role play involving a client and a counselor. I
suggest role play (as structured here) rather than chair work when the student counselor is verbally stuck; he or she simply doesn't know what to
say to the client. Also, I find that chair work is indicated when the student
counselor knows what she or he wants to say, but hasn't yet said it for a
variety of reasons. In the roleplay, the instructor or practicum supervisor
invites the student to play the client, since the student knows the client
dynamics directly. The student is usually able to model her or his perception of the client quite readily and often inadvertently demonstrates many
key dynamics of the relationship that emerge out of his or her own frustration, anger, or bewilderment. The student teaches the class and the instructor about the behaviors of her or his client and shows the instructor/super-
visor how to "be" that client when time for role reversal arrives. The instructor, in turn, while playing the counselor, offers alternative counselor
behaviors for the student to experience, consider, and eventually practice
when he or she plays the counselor in the role reversal. Following the role-
play, the heart of the constructivist dimension occurs — open discourse to
facilitate the construction of new meanings and possibilities for both the
student counselor and the client. The role-play may be conceptualized in
three parts: prologue, dialogue, and epilogue.

I.   Prologue

A.   Introduce students to the possibility of further exploring something
     they just said about the client (or some known issues the student/su-
     pervisee has with her or his client) in greater depth via role play.

B.   Ask their permission

     1). If they refuse or seem reluctant, ask if they have further questions
     about role plays and their limits. Consider offering them a gentle chal-
     lenge to take a step beyond talking *about* their issue and moving into
     discovery via immersion *in* it. If they are still reluctant, accept this and
     process their reluctance or rejection of the idea. Such exploration alone

will often open up new areas for consideration, such as students' hypotheses regarding self or the client.

2). If they agree:

– Explain the set-up. They will play the *client*; you will play *them.*

– Ask the student to explain a typical situation in which he or she feels stuck, intimidated, belittled, or dissatisfied, or if she is a pre-practicum student, which he or she imagines (his or her "worst nightmare" situation, or their fantasized "client from hell"). What they offer here can be used as an opening in the dialogue section below.

– Ask them to take a minute to imagine they themselves as the client, assuming the client's manner and attitude, and to signal you when they are ready.

II. Dialogue

A. Begin the exchange by having the student-as-client offer one of the responses which typically causes the student-as-counselor a problem. Next, model alternative counselor interventions, which respect both parties. Continue as long as the exchange has energy.

B. Process this first exchange with questions, for example: "How was it for you to be your client?" "What did you learn about him/her?" "How realistic was my portrayal of you with the new responses?" "Which of my responses had the most impact and why?" "Which of them could you imagine yourself saying?" Other students may contribute their own observations at this time or later after the entire role reversal has been completed. Following the student's offering, present some of your perceptions of them as client, and of yourself playing them.

C. Ask them if they would be willing to reverse roles.

1). If they refuse, offer a gentle, respectful challenge to take the next step and apply what they have just experienced. If they still refuse, bring closure by facilitating a discussion of what they can conclude from the experience, and what hypotheses and meanings can be derived from your shared observations.

2). If they agree, repeat steps II (A and B above). This time, they practice some of the counselor modeling they observed in you, while you accurately play the client whose behavior has just been modeled for you. Once again, they precede you in any processing that occurs so as to maximize their participation in the co-exploration and co-discovery.

D. If they are willing, and it seems valuable, continue the dialogue, while giving them additional practice of their new behaviors to build and test other hypotheses.

III. Epilogue

After the dialogical exchanges are complete, instructors with a constructivist orientation can offer students a rich opportunity to explore their experiences and co-construct hypotheses for application to this particular counseling relationship and others. For example, students may report significant shifts in their perspectives regarding either their clients or themselves. Sometimes they discover increased empathic understandings about the life experiences of their client, such as reactions based on fear, guilt, or sadness. They may also discover countertransferential dynamics evoked by the role-play and may need to process related emotions. Yet another benefit is they may realize that they can *feel* and *express* emotions previously blocked in this or in other relationships.

Gestalt Chair Work

Gestalt chair work, an experiential "cousin" of role play, provides students with the opportunity to explore *intra*personal (usually the client's) as well as *inter*personal issues. In the intrapersonal domain, students (as clients) can play both poles of a client's internal dilemma. In the interpersonal domain, when the student counselor herself experiences an impasse in the relationship with a client, she can play both persons in the conflicted therapeutic dyad. Thus both inner and outer protagonists can be portrayed experientially. As noted above in the role-play section, a key indicator for choosing chair work over role play is how uncertain the student is about initiating the simulated dialogue. I advocate using chair work when students already know what they want to say to themselves or to the client (in cases of external conflict), but have not yet risked it because of lack of trust in their own instincts, or because of uncertainty (or fear) of the client's response. Chair work, like role playing, can be portrayed through the same three stages of prologue, dialogue, and epilogue.

I.   Prologue

A. and B. Student exchanges with the chair

    1). Conduct as above in Role Reversal Role Play.

    2). If they agree,

    – Explain the set-up (she or he will dialogue with the other pole or person placed in an empty chair),

    – Ask the student to explain a typical situation in which she or he feels the intra- or interpersonal impasse (confusion, stuckness, fear, intimidation),

    – Supply an empty chair and allow the student to place it where desired (note the chair's position and distance for debriefing purposes in the Epilogue portion).

    – Ask her or him to take a minute to imagine the other pole or person in the chair, to silently note any of its features and their own reaction(s), and to signal you when they are ready. NOTE: Sometimes this will be as far as the student is willing to proceed. If so, there is usually ample material to debrief at this point.

II. Dialogue

A. When they are ready, ask them what they would like to say to _____ (hereafter referring to the other pole of themselves as the client or the other person with whom they are experiencing difficulty). Have them speak from their original chair, speaking for either pole (if the conflict is intrapersonal) or for themselves as the counselor (if the issue is interpersonal with their client). Watch them closely and allow a pause or two if necessary in their opening statement. Watch to see when the energy drops noticeably (they will often look at you, with verbal or nonverbal messages indicating "That's it" or "Now What?").

B. Ask them if they would be okay being ____ (the other pole or person) and responding from the other chair. Here again, a supportive challenge may be all that an uncertain student needs. If they decline the invitation, then respect their decision and process the experience with them. In open discussion, without coercion or preconceived conclusions, see what meaning(s) can be co-developed.

C. If they accept the invitation to play the other pole or person, motion them to the empty chair. Allow them the time they need to get started, also allowing a pause or two during their portrayal, and, as in step "A" above, note the eventual drop in energy when they seem to have finished.

D. Invite them back to the original chair to continue the dialogue, allowing pauses, and noting the eventual energy drop.

E. Continue the chair shifting for at least two exchanges if possible, or for as long as it continues naturally, motioning them from chair to chair if needed.

NOTE: 1) Some students are willing to dialogue but either do not wish to change chairs, or find it too artificial, distracting, or cumbersome. In this case, they may dialogue sitting in the same chair, shifting positions or using their two hands to house the "voices." 2) Some coaching may be helpful, that is, repeating statements the student has already offered, or encouraging the student to repeat key phrases. Also note emotions the student expresses non-verbally and perhaps urge the student to express them in words. I also find it helpful on occasion to offer encouragement, like, "Take your time", or "I know this is difficult, saying what has been bottled up for so long."

F. Finish the chair work after checking in with them about when they feel finished.

III. Epilogue

A. Ask them to go to a *neutral* location (free of any residual emotion from either pole or person played) and describe their experience of being in *each* chair: "When I was here . . . ." or "In this chair, I . . . . " Note that this interim processing step in a neutral location is not employed in the debriefing of role play activity.

B. Offer any observations or experiences *you* have/had regarding them in each location or of their observations made from the neutral location.

C. Invite them back to their original location to reflect on the entire experience (feelings, impressions, learnings). Here instructors offer their observations, impressions, and experiences and continue the dialogue, seeking meanings similarly to the final step of the role play epilogue above.

CONCLUSION

Both of these experiential activities require the development of trust as a prerequisite and time to process afterward. Either activity can easily develop into a 15-20 minute process. The epilogue alone often requires the majority of this time. Given sufficient trust, "equity" in the relationship, and adequate time for debriefing, the possibilities for hypothesis generating and meaning making are seemingly limitless. Enjoy the adventure.

REFERENCES

Bandler, R., & Grinder, J. (1979). *Frogs into princes: Neuro linguistic programming.* Moab, UT: Real People Press.

Corey, G. (1996a). *Theory and practice of counseling and psychotherapy* (5th ed.). Pacific Grove, CA: Brooks/Cole.

Corey, G (1996b). *Student manual for theory and practice of counseling and psychotherapy* (5th ed.). Pacific Grove, CA: Brooks/Cole.

Freire, P. (1971). *Pedagogy of the oppressed.* New York: Herder and Herder.

Kegan, R. (1994). *In over our heads.* Cambridge, MA: Harvard University Press.

Kolb, D. (1984). *Experiential learning: Experience as the source of learning and development.* Englewood Cliffs, NJ: Prentice Hall.

Lazarus, A. A. (1989). *The practice of multimodal therapy.* Baltimore: Johns Hopkins University Press.

Lovell, C. & McAuliffe, G. J. (1997). Principles of constructivist training and education. In T. L. Sexton & B. L. Griffin (Eds.), *Constructivist thinking in counseling practice, research, and training,* (pp. 221-223). New York: Teachers College.

McAuliffe, G., & Lovell, C. (2000). Encouraging transformation: Guidelines for constructivist and developmental instruction. In G. McAuliffe, K. Eriksen, and Associates, *Preparing counselors and therapists: Creating constructivist and developmental programs,* (pp.14-41). Alexandria, VA: Association for Counselor Education and Supervision.

Sexton, T. L. & B. L. Griffin (Eds.). (1997). *Constructivist thinking in counseling practice, research, and training.* New York: Teachers College.

MODELING THE COUNSELING INTERVIEW IN THREE STAGES: A COURSE-OPENING ACTIVITY
—*Garrett McAuliffe*

At a recent national counseling convention, panelists at a session on the teaching of counseling reported that, above all, students wished to see their instructors demonstrate counseling skills. It was noted that many instructors do not do so. Perhaps this is because we fear making mistakes. Perhaps our clinical experience lies so far in the past that we distrust our skills. Perhaps we are concerned about being too good, intimidating the novices in the room. Maybe many of us are introverts who don't like being "on stage." To these reasons, I respond with the well-coined phrase, "Just do it."

The arguments for us to be fellow actors in the classroom role-play drama are compelling. Vicarious learning is clearly a powerful vehicle for skill acquisition, as the social learning research has shown (Bandura, 1986). Demonstration also is an inductive way to illustrate the complexity of counseling, the multiple directions that might be taken on the counseling journey. During demonstrations, we expose the complexity of the counseling enterprise and challenge any illusions of the dualist in all of us that there is a simple recipe for counseling. When we pause during the demonstration, or during a tape of it, we can share our hunches, our musings, our struggles, and our doubts a la the Interpersonal Process Recall approach of Norman Kagan (1980). Sharing such doubts is a too-rare commodity among instructors, as the liberatory and feminist educators have reminded us (e.g. Freire, 1994; Schmiedewind, 1987). So, in demonstrations, we invite students to join the community of doubters and ponderers, to reflect with us on the evolution of good practice.

The triple enactment of the counseling interview presented here can be particularly effective during the initial session of a course. On the affective level, it might comfort students to see the professor on the spot, sweating and vulnerable as both client and counselor. On the intellectual level, students might see science at work: They and we induce possibilities from concrete experience and observation. We observe, deliberate, weigh, decide, act, and observe again.

Another function of this triple enactment might be called its "advance organizer" function; that is, the activity communicates that this course will require activity, that we will all be counselors and clients together in this course. Finally, the activity builds community: Students participate, laugh, feel, and think with the instructor, and get to know one another early. Such an outcome is not to be winked at: Today, as I write this piece, a former student has just told me that in the counseling skills course he felt more supported, even embraced, as a gay man than in any other in his program of study. The following activity may have contributed to his experience.

Objectives

- To offer an overview of the choices and behaviors in counseling.

- To prepare students for the activities to come in the course.

- To build trust among classmates and between the students and the instructor.

- To model personal disclosure and introspection within the personal comfort limits of participants.

- To model the role play-and-critique protocol that will be used in the course.

Description of the Activity

There are three phases in this activity.

I. *Instructor as client.*

Introductory remarks. In the very opening moments of the first class of the course, the instructor sits among the students and says, "I'd like to begin by telling you a story. It is about what is going on with me. I'd like you to listen and to do what seems helpful. You are all participants. Just chime in with what seems important to say or do as I talk." For later processing, it is helpful if the session is videotaped.

The interview. The instructor then proceeds to tell of a personal situation or issue, one that she or he, of course, feels comfortable disclosing at this early juncture of the class. The instructor should pause regularly, allowing the silence to sit, letting students ponder their inclinations before they respond with what they consider helpful. Students are asked to chime in in any way that seems helpful at the moment, either in turn or as the spirit moves them.

During-session processing. After about fifteen minutes, the instructor ends the session and asks the students what it was like to be in the role of "helper." The instructor asks: "What were you feeling? Thinking? What were you trying to do? What did you like that happened? What do you think was going on with the interviewee and her or his situation?" Thus begins the reflexivity and introspection that will be needed for becoming a good counselor.

Post-session processing. The instructor writes two column headings on the board: "What's Going On?" and "What Did You Do?" These categories represent "client conceptualization" and "counseling intervention," respectively. They are the two key meta-dimensions of all of counseling work and are constant themes of the course. The tape of the session is then played. The instructor pauses the tape at a number of points and asks students what they think is/was going on with the interviewee. Each student might first individually write down her or his speculations about the instructor-client's situation. The instructor then asks students to share ideas, and writes them on the board in the first column (above). As they review the tape, the instructor also notes on the board, under the second question, each intervention that the students provided, giving the interventions skill labels such as "Open Question" or "Advice." The instructor notes, even counts, the types of skills used. Such is the portent, or advance organizer, of things to come.

II. Instructor as counselor.

Instructor interviews. Now the roles switch. The instructor asks for a volunteer to be interviewed about anything she or he wishes to talk about. The two sit in the middle of the class circle, and the instructor counsels the student. Again they tape the session if possible (or a recorder notes the interventions).

Immediate three-part processing. After about ten minutes, the instructor stops the session and asks the interviewee about her or his experience of being interviewed. Such a question models the constructivist notion that the meaning that each of us makes is a central concern – in this case, the client's meaning making is held up as primary. Then the instructor-counselor shares her or his feelings and internal deliberations during and after the interview. Finally, the class shares their feedback and questions about the interview. Thus the instructor prepares the class for the "triadic" activity that will be the core of the course – client and counselor participate in counseling, observer observes the session, and then all three offer their thoughts and opinions on the practice session.

Review of the tape. The tape of the session is played and paused at selected moments (or, if the session is not taped, the students' notes about the interventions that were used are shared). The instructor labels the types of interventions she or he used. Then, in order to evoke "case conceptualization," students are asked to write down their speculations on "What's Going On?" (with the client and his or her situation). These are discussed in all of their variety – cultural issues, psychodynamics, relationship factors, faulty thinking, systems issues, and more. Usually at this moment the contrast becomes apparent between the first enactment — that is, the class's question-and-advice-heavy interviewing approach—and the second enactment—that is, the instructor's reflective and empathic interviewing manner. Students immediately see a person-centered alternative for helping, one in which empathy is powerful. A light may dawn on the possibility of being empathic and allowing others to make their own meanings as at least one way to help. They may begin to understand that they need not be such forceful directors of the counseling drama.

III. Students counsel each other.

The third enactment follows (usually after a break). Students form triads and interview each other for ten minutes each, with one student acting as observer each time. They follow the triadic model that has been demonstrated. When the students return to the large group after their "baseline" sessions, they are usually energized but exhausted. "Such hard work!" "What do you say?" "Ten minutes is so long!" are usually among their comments as we process the experience. They have entered the "hot seat" for the first of many times in the course. They have experienced the choice points; they honor the complexity. As the students share their experiences in the large group, we begin to become a community of learner-teacher-inquirers. It becomes clear that emotions will be allowed in this room. Doubt will be honored. We will be held by each other. But we will also try, risk, and dare to be wrong, while all the time caring and honoring our felt lives.

The instructor uses the rest of the class session to talk about the nature of the course, connecting it to this activity. Students are thus "warned" about what is to come. This activity usually takes a full two-and-a-half-hour class session. The syllabus can wait – they will read it and come in with comments and questions the next time. For now, they have begun the work of counseling.

REFERENCES

Bandura, A. (1986). *Social foundations of thought and action: A social-cognitive theory.* Englewood Cliffs, NJ: Prentice-Hall.

Freire, P. (1994). *Pedagogy of the oppressed.* New York: Continuum.

Kagan, N. (1980) *Interpersonal process recall: A method of influencing human interaction.* ERIC Doc ED 017946.

Schniedewind, N. (1987). Feminist values: Guidelines for teaching methodology in Women's Studies. In Shor, I. (Ed.), *Friere for the classroom* (pp. 170-179). New York: Boynton/Cook.

6

In-Class Group Activities

Karen Eriksen, Gail Uellendahl,

Joan Blacher, and Garrett McAuliffe

Group work reflects the "real world" communal context of most of our lives: that is, we live in family groups, work groups, friendship groups, and other teams. Through classroom group work, we encourage students to pay attention to their interpersonal behavior. They can then find effective relational skills validated or can work on changing ineffective patterns. Group work punctuates the need for cooperative work habits, which are particularly important for students who are inclined to be overly autonomous or, on the other side, too adherent and obsequious. Group experiences become beneficial when accompanied by introspection and processing of group dynamics.

Group work can also instigate development. Through seeing peers contribute to knowledge and by watching ideas emerge in dialogue, students may reduce their reliance on authorities. That is, group work can counter the tendency for students to assign to the instructor the sole role of expert and knowledge-giver. In the following group activities, namely the card sort exercise, the debate activity, and the case study strategy, students challenge each other to come up with solutions to difficult and sometimes controversial problems. They participate in decision making, consensus building, and conflict resolution.

Other advantages emerge from utilizing group work in a class. In groups, students can practice skills with each other, efficiently using the peer group for feedback and as a sounding board for ideas. Participating in a group activity is energizing, especially in the context of the typical two-and-a-half hour evening graduate counseling class. Lastly, many students will "find their voice," that is, literally speak, in the safety of a small group while not being able to do so in the often-intimidating large class setting.

In order that in-class groups might serve their learning and developmental purposes, the following guidelines should be implemented:

- *The maximum size of group that seems workable for full participation is eight to ten, although this can vary.*

- *Groups might be formed at random, by ability, common interest in a topic, or by demographics (for example, hetero- or homogeneous assignment by gender, ethnicity, or age). The assignment strategy will affect the students' experiences.*

- *Norms should be discussed; for instance, no name-calling or "put-downs;" focus on ideas rather than a person or his or her character when correcting mistakes; listen and try to accept diverse ideas instead of rejecting others' contributions; watch your own "air time."*

- *Formal roles—observer, facilitator, timekeeper, recorder—can be given and later discussed to promote efficiency and development.*

- *Give clear directions; be clear on the time allowed for the activity.*

- *Pay attention to the physical environment; members should be arranged so that they can see each other; separate groups so that the noise level doesn't interfere with the work.*

- *Finally, move around to groups, help to keep them on-task, and remind them of the time left.*

—Garrett McAuliffe

INTRODUCTORY CARD SORT[1] EXERCISE
—Karen Eriksen

The constructivist educator encourages students to participate in defining the learning process as well as the learning content. Such an inclusive impulse emerges from the belief that students possess valuable information from their own life experiences. Further, openness to student input serves an educational purpose: Students develop their own ideas (hooks, 1994) and take responsibility for their own learning experiences (Kegan, 1982, 1994). The "Introductory Card Sort Exercise" communicates such constructivist ideas from the first class meeting. During the exercise, students individually list their expectations for the course on "cards" and then work together with other students to develop consensus about the directions of the course.

The exercise is based on such classroom norms as expecting student participation, inviting student contributions, celebrating student decision making, and actively co-constructing the learning process. The results of such norms are that community and camaraderie building begin from the outset: Students talk with each other right away, actively collaborate on decisions, and compromise in the process of building consensus. Finally, when students participate in this way, the professor has the opportunity to observe the group process, to assess roles that different students might take, and to determine which students are natural leaders and which students might need to be encouraged to voice their opinions.

Including this exercise at the beginning of my courses has benefited the course in other ways as well. The initial class period is no longer a "throw away" introductory session in which students passively receive the course description and requirements. It becomes a lively, energetic discussion of expectations and desires. Students are often pleasantly surprised at the degree of concurrence between their ideas and those of the instructor. And where less concurrence exists, students and instructor begin the dialogue about what will work best for this group of students. Students also often express surprise when the instructor changes portions of the syllabus in response to their suggestions. Such responsiveness is particularly helpful in the internship course, as such responsiveness to student needs allows "holes" in the prior curriculum to be filled at a time when students most need it—as they begin to practice.

A side benefit is that students reflect on how they function in groups, groups that are not primarily process groups. Group members often joke with one another about how one side got their way or how perhaps not everyone was heard. They also joke about "cheating." This seems to mean that they have rephrased their ideas to be more inclusive, or have tried to find unusual ways to merge two ideas together so as to be able to include both in the requisite number (which of course I consider a bonus, not cheating). This sort of group discovery clearly foreshadows the sorts of demands that will be placed on students in the work world when they will be expected to participate collegially on projects.

Objectives

- Introduce the course to the students.

- Introduce the students to each other.

- Communicate to the students the importance of their co-creating the learning experience.

- Gain student input on the course.

Description of the Activity

The instructor begins the exercise by distributing six index cards to each student. Each student spends five minutes writing one idea per card about what he or she believes ought to happen in the class. Students' ideas may be based on:

- their understanding of the course topic

- their particular content needs

- an awareness of what they have not yet experienced in the program, but feel a need to experience

- other ideas relevant to the course, the program, or the particular university

- their preferred learning style

Next, students divide into dyads for five minutes to discuss their ideas and to decide together on six of those ideas that they believe to be most important (this means that they reduced their original twelve ideas to six joint ideas). This pair then meets with another pair for five minutes to repeat the process: that is, narrowing their twelve ideas to the "six most important." Then two foursomes join to do the same. Thus, what began as six ideas per student has now become six ideas per group of eight students. The eight-student groups also decide on how they would like introduce themselves to each other and then to the class.

After introductions, the groups of eight present their ideas to the rest of the class. The instructor writes the ideas on the board, clarifying, adding suggestions, and punctuating which—in his or her view—are critical elements. Finally, to encourage student attention to class interactions, the instructor leads a discussion on what the exercise was like for the class members, how they reached decisions, what it took to achieve consensus, how they incorporated diverse views, and whether they felt comfortable with the process.

Spaces may be left in the syllabus until after this exercise is completed, so that student contributions may augment the instructor's ideas. Questions to be answered on the index cards may be changed to fit the particular needs of the professor, the class, and the setting. Numbers of cards per student may be changed depending on the final number of suggestions desired and the class time available for the exercise.

NOTE

1.   Adapted from Joe Greenberg's exercise, demonstrated in *Teaching Strategies for Adult Learners*, a course taught at George Washington University, Washington DC, 1995.

REFERENCES

hooks, b. (1994). *Teaching to transgress.* New York: Routledge.

Kegan, R. (1982). *The evolving self.* Cambridge, MA: Harvard University Press.

Kegan, R. (1994). *In over our heads.* Cambridge, MA: Harvard University Press.

THE GREAT DEBATE[1]
—Karen Eriksen

Constructivist educators actively engage both the hearts and minds of students, designing activities that meet individual students at their respective developmental levels. In "The Great Debate," students experience different sides of an important issue, think critically about the controversy, and voice their perspectives "pro" or "con."

A value of this exercise lies in the evidence that active knowledge creation and emotional arousal, in this case through debate, bring content to life; this in turn increases retention (Caine and Caine, 1994). Debates on issues that students care about and will need to consider in their future employment settings encourage the investment of their emotions, as well as of their minds. As a result, I have found that students explore the issues independently after the course has ended. Also, debates give students the opportunity to hear multiple perspectives. The instructor encourages all students to voice their opinions and give evidence. Students bring outside experiences into the learning environment, experiences that inform the learning of others. Further, although students experience the same reading material prior to the debate, they interact with that material differently based on "lenses" they have developed from growing up in different contexts. Thus, students gain first-hand experience of the "construction" of knowledge.

Students may also progress developmentally as a result of debates. Initially, they find themselves very passionate in expressing their positions. However, when their peers express opposite positions, they find themselves considering, sometimes for the first time, the notion that absolutes may not exist. They find themselves thinking more carefully about the issues, considering that many answers may exist, and struggling with what stance they might take with respect to the issue.

A word of caution: More dualistic (Perry, 1970) students may consider debates an opportunity for "winning" or "strong arming" the opposition. They may enthusiastically dominate the "chairs" during the debate, making it difficult for other opinions to be expressed. If allowed, these students might alienate the rest of the class, creating a hostle atmosphere, rather than a safe environment in which different perspectives can be openly considered. In order to prevent the development of such an unhelpful learning environment, instructors with more dualistic students in their classes may want to avoid debates as a teaching strategy. Or they may need to stop the debate and ask the class to process what is happening, challenging the students to reclaim a more helpful atmosphere.

Because debate is useful for developing critical thinking, becoming aware of multiple perspectives, and discussing controversial issues, many counseling courses could benefit from debating strategies. For example, in Theories of Counseling, "Dr. Freud" and "Dr. Glasser" (or other theoretical fathers and mothers) could debate the most helpful treatment for a client. In Ethics or Professional Issues courses, students might debate the different sides of such ethical dilemmas as keeping confidentiality (or not) with HIV positive clients who reveal that they are having unprotected sex with a partner, to report (or not) a boss who is behaving unethically, or to refer (or not) a family whose child is in trouble and whose father's fundamentalism makes it impossible for the child (or the counselor) to connect with him.

In Multicultural Counseling, students might debate the benefits/problems of individualism or the ways to treat drug addiction from the points of view of different cultures. In Introduction to Counseling, debate topics might include the pros and cons of managed care or licensure, the inclusion of substance abuse prevention courses in schools (or any other professional issue which might be contested within the profession or between profession members and other members of society). In Human Development, the class could hold a debate on a moral issue, with one side representing people from one developmental stage and the other side representing people from another developmental stage.

Objectives

- Involve students in advocating for different sides of a controversial issue.

- Generate awareness of the multiple perspectives on the issue.

- Encourage students to find their own voices.

- Offer students the opportunity for critical thinking and personal decision making concerning issues pertinent to their eventual practice.

- Stimulate critical thinking skills that are generalizable to decision making about other difficult issues.

Description of the Activity

Students read material from two sides of a controversial issue during the week prior to the debate. For instance, for "The Great Prozac Debate," they might read selections from *Talking Back to Prozac*, by Peter Breggin, and *Listening to Prozac*, by Peter Kramer. For "The Great Managed Care Debate," they might read from *Breaking Free of Managed Care*, by Dana

Ackley, and *How to Partner with Managed Care,* by Browning and Browning.

During the debate, students sit in a circle around four centered chairs. Two of the middle chairs are placed side-by-side facing two other side-by-side chairs. One side takes the "pro" position and the other side takes the "con" position; in the Prozac debate, one side is "for" the use of Prozac and the other side is "against" the use of Prozac.

The instructor asks two people to take "permanent" pro and con positions by occupying two of the chairs facing each other. The other two chairs are left empty. The two "permanent" debaters begin with opening statements and maintain their positions for most of the debate. Then members of the class voluntarily come forward one-by-one as they are inspired to contribute. They sit in the remaining pro or con chairs, and voice their perspectives. Class members are only allowed to offer their perspectives when sitting in one of the middle chairs. The instructor can also take one of the empty chairs at key moments, sometimes on the pro side and other times on the con side. The ability of the instructor to take opposing positions communicates the complexity of the controversy and challenges students to give full credence to the varying perspectives expressed. And so the debate continues until everyone has had a chance to voice his or her ideas, and until the issue has been exhausted. The professor then leads a brief discussion about what was learned in the process.

NOTE

1. Created with Bill Bruck, Marymount University, 1995

REFERENCES

Ackley, D. C. (1999). *Breaking free of managed care.* New York: Guilford.

Breggin, P. R. (1994). *Talking back to Prozac.* New York: St. Martin's Press

Browning, C. H., & Browning, B. J. (1996). *How to partner with managed care: A "do-it-yourself kit" for building working relationships & getting steady referrals.* New York: John Wiley & Sons.

Caine, R. N. & Caine, G. (1994). *Making connections: Teaching and the human brain.* Menlo Park, CA: Addison-Wesley.

Kramer, P. D. *Listening to Prozac.* (1997). New York: Viking Penguin.

Perry, W. (1970). *Forms of intellectual and ethical development in the college years.* New York: Holt, Rinehart, and Winston.

CREATING A PROGRAM
—Karen Eriksen

Groans and looks of confusion usually greet me when I announce an in-class assignment that asks students to create a program of some sort by using the course information they have been introduced to thus far. Initially, many times after a long day of work, the hope that "class won't be too challenging tonight" meets the inherent messiness of such an experiential activity, turning into reluctance and resignation. As class progresses, however, messiness turns to hope, resignation turns to excitement, reluctance turns into passion, and a community of learners and program developers is born. Their excitement mounts, as they struggle together in small groups to turn the "usual" treatment models into something unique and innovative. Their sense seems to shift in the direction of, "Now we are really doing something that we can use out in the real world." This segment offers three program creation activities that might be used in a human development course. I then discuss how the activities might be expanded into other courses.

The "Creating a Program" activity offers students an inductive and active approach to applying principles of human development while learning about psychoeducation and other program development. Students apply principles learned in class to a real-world need and systematically develop a program.

The activity also builds on principles established by research on adult learning. That is, knowledge is created in a small group of students who, in the process of working together, might become a community. During such community building, students have to address the usual struggles that face team members who are trying to work together. This includes difficulties such as the following: members who don't seem to be contributing; work and learning styles that differ; choices about leadership; conflicts that need resolving; anticipation of judgement by some external authority; decisions about how best to access the knowledge and experience resources of diverse members; how best to hear everyone's voice.

Students also struggle together with other students to figure out how "book learning" and lectures might realistically be enacted in the world. The close relationship between the classroom and the real world allows students' knowledge creation to be closely related to their professional— and sometimes their personal—goals.

Adult learning principles, when applied, increase adult learners' motivation to learn and their retention of learning for future use. In addition, following such principles may promote the emergence of students' voices, their capacity to rely on their own authority for making decisions, their confidence in their own meaning making and knowledge creation. Such a developmental leap is called moving from reliance on "convention" to reliance on "conscientiousness" by Loevinger (1976), from "received" or "subjective knowing" to "procedural knowing" by Belenky, Clinchy, Goldberger, and Tarule (1986), and from an "interpersonal" to an "institutional order of consciousness" by Kegan (1994).

Other courses might also benefit from the Creating a Program activity. For instance, in the Introductory or Professional Issues course, students might create an advocacy program or a program to update school counselors' knowledge about ethical decision making. In Counseling Theories, students might develop an Adlerian parenting program or a wellness program that uses any other theory as its foundation. In Diagnosis and Treatment Planning, students might develop a treatment program for clients who share a common diagnosis or a program to prevent—after assessing early warning signs—the full development of a diagnosable problem. In an Understanding Addictions course, students might design an innovative substance abuse treatment program or a prison program to prevent recidivism. In a Career Development course, students might design a program for new college students who are having trouble deciding on a major. The possibilities are many for each of the courses that are typically taught in counseling programs.

Objectives

Students will:

- Apply reading and lecture information to meeting a real world need.

- Systematically walk through the steps of program development.

- Engage in building a community of learners and knowledge creators.

Description of the Activities

Activity I: After students have walked through the stages of infancy, early childhood, and middle childhood, encountering textbook material that clearly points to early warning signs for later difficulties, the instructor hands out the following instructions and questions to small groups of 4 or 5 students:

Early Intervention and Parenting Program

As you read in the chapters related to infancy and childhood, many problems may be prevented if early warning signs are heeded. Therefore, your job is to design an early intervention and parenting program that will heed those warning signs. You are in leadership in an elementary/preschool combination school in downtown Santa Ana, California. Many of your students/families are Hispanic or Vietnamese and from the lower socioeconomic levels. You have applied for grant money to design this program and now have a year to design and implement it. There are two parts to this program:

Assessment:

- What problems might be precluded if early warning signs were heeded?

- Therefore, what early warning signs will you look for?

- How will you assess their presence?

Parenting/Family Training:

- Design a parent education program to be delivered at various times during preschool and elementary school.

- What are your goals/objectives (ie, what problems are you trying to prevent and what steps/approaches will you take to prevent them)?

- What components will you include in your program and why? (ie, what sorts of programming will reduce later risks?)

- How will you assure/encourage wide participation by those in need?

- How will you assure that families generalize what is learned in the program into everyday practice?

Activity II: After students have engaged materials about adolescence, encountering textbook material about problems that teens face, developmental needs of teens, parental roles in teen lives, and the causes and results of interrupted development, the instructor hands out the following instructions and questions to small groups of 4 or 5 students:

Residential Counselor Exercise

You are a residential counselor working together with a team of other counselors, teens, and administrators to develop an innovative foster care group home for adolescents. You have been selected because you are a counselor and those who want to develop the program recognize the unique contributions counselors have to make. Your job is to represent the unique perspectives of the counseling profession – education, promotion of development, attention to the whole child, recognition of systemic and contextual factors in behavior – as you all work together to design a program to meet the special needs of this population group. Your small group represents the counselors working on this team. You are meeting to gather your thoughts about how to create the best possible program. As you develop your thoughts into an organized "program."

1. Consider the needs of this population group and what problems the adolescents are likely to be facing.

2. Be comprehensive in addressing all of the areas of development we have read about thusfar.

3. Develop goals for your program.

4. Consider programmatic ways (objectives) to best promote development and remediate the problems of these teens. Include all of the above philosophies that counselors usually represent.

5. Consider who besides the teens you would want to include in your program.

6. Consider what sort of staff would best be able to institute your program.

7. Plan for "after the program" needs as well, so as to anticipate how you will need to prepare the teens for discharge from the group home.

8. Explain/justify/give evidence or support for each part of your plan.

9. Organize your thoughts into a proposal for the larger group

At this point, you need not consider how the program will be funded as that will be the job of the larger, multidisciplinary group.

––––––

Activity III: After students have encountered coursework related to human beings' progression through adulthood, aging, and death and dying, coursework in which successful aging is clearly connected to planning ahead, the instructor hands out the following instructions and questions to small groups of 4 or 5 students:

Prevention Program for Those Becoming Old

As was clear in this week's chapters, many problems we typically associate with aging are preventable and thus do not actually have to be experienced by those who are aging. Therefore, your job as a new counselor is to design a primary/secondary prevention program related to the problems of aging. Make sure to address the needs of elders in different socioeconomic groups and of different races/ethnicities. Begin with the assumption that you have as much money as you need, and can design the ideal program. After designing the ideal, work backwards to prioritize program components based on more limited income. You have grant money to design and implement this program. There are two parts to this program:

Assessment:

• For the secondary prevention part of program, what early warning signs will you look for?

• How will you assess their presence?

Prevention Program:

• Design a comprehensive primary and secondary prevention program for problems related to aging.

• What are your goals/objectives? What areas will you address?

• What program components will you include and why? (what sorts of programming will reduce later risks?)

• What teaching/counseling strategies will be most effective?

• At what age will you begin the program? Why?

• How will you assure/encourage wide participation by those in need?

• How will you ensure generalization/application of curriculum to real life?

———

During the activity and after. I generally allow a full class session—really a very small amount of time — for students to create their programs. While they work, I wander from group to group, listening, posing questions, offering support and information, challenging students to think creatively and to bring all that they are to the creation. During the last 45 minutes of class, we process their work. I ask them to take 10 minutes to present the highlights of their programs to one another. They are often amazed at how different the programs look and are enthusiastic about including other groups' ideas in their own programs. I then finish class by asking questions such as: "What was this experience like for you?" "What was the one most important thing you learned as a result of this activity?" "What will you take with you out into your work as a professional counselor?" "What problems did you encounter during your work together?" "How might you resolve such problems for future work?" Finally, for homework, the small groups write up their programs and email them to the rest of the class. Individually, students then consider the work of the other groups and decide which ideas they believe might enrich their own group's program. They then compose their own personal programmatic ideas into a written paper that is subsequently submitted to the instructor.

CONCLUSION

Recently, when my students participated in Activity I, I was pleased with the increased social concern that the students showed. I was impressed with the seriousness with which they approached the task, the genuine concern I saw about the poor and disenfranchised, about those who without such concern might slip through the cracks of our mental health services systems. I was also impressed with the students' genuine concern with the multi-ethnicity of the target population. For example, many of the student groups struggled for a long time to figure out how they could manage the language barrier in a way that was possible, meaningful, and inclusive, so that all who were willing could genuinely participate. They found that the language issue was not an easy problem to fix. Their struggles seemed to, for one evening, match the struggles experienced by the people themselves whose first language is not English.

I was also impressed with the process. Great benefits emerged from having a multidisciplinary team work on the project: For instance, some people knew about schools, some knew about interpreters and aides in classrooms, some knew about juvenile justice systems, some could see the advantages that churches might have in reaching people. So, even if they weren't professionals yet, they all clearly had knowledge resources to draw upon. A collaborative mentality has been demonstrated.

The students also struggled with logistics of program delivery. How would they put all of their goals together into a focused meaningful experience? How would they recruit people to come? How could the leaders remove enough obstacles that the people who really needed the program would be there? For instance, how could the planners work around potential participants' work schedules? How would they avoid overwhelming the participants, and yet involve them enough so that change could occur? So struggling with logistics naturally led to discussions about incentives for people to work on change.

As is probably obvious at this point, students "Creating a Program" faced, in an abbreviated form, many of the experiences they would most likely face when out in the field. Their idealism met some daunting logistical realities. They faced obstacles that would take work to overcome. They saw the benefits of hearing multiple perspectives when planning. They were faced with what they didn't know, while also recognizing how much they already had to contribute.

Perhaps they could not find answers to all of the problems or group process issues, but they did come face to face with the questions. And in that fact might lie a significant benefit of this activity: To create a readiness to learn, an awareness of the gaps in one's knowledge, and an outline to fill in during the rest of one's graduate program.

REFERENCES

Belenky, M., Clinchy, B., Goldberger, N., & Tarule, J. (1986). *Women's ways of knowing*. New York: Basic Books.

Kegan, R. (1982) *The evolving self*. Cambridge, MA: Harvard University Press.

Kegan, R. (1994). *In over our heads: The mental demands of modern life*. Cambridge: Harvard University Press.

Loevinger, J. (1976). *Ego development: Conceptions and theories*. San Francisco: Jossey-Bass.

THE INTERNSHIP CASE SUPERVISION GO-ROUND
—*Garrett McAuliffe*

One of the values of an internship or practicum seminar is the empowerment of learners. Haag-Granello's (1999) work has shown the internship to be easily the most powerful development-instigating experience in a counseling curriculum. Much of that is due to the testing-and-reflection of the daily field experience, the inductive-deductive dance of trying out theory and creating new, personal theory-in-action.

But development is not automatic and "doing" is not the only key dimension in learning, contrary to the wisdom of the Chinese proverb ("In the doing is the learning."). It is in the "reflection on the doing" that much learning occurs. It is our task as counselor educators to instigate such reflection. The internship can do just that, through journal-writing, field supervisory conversations, and, as shown here, in the case presentation dimension of the internship seminar.

What is described below is a variation on a classic empowerment-oriented career decision-making activity. Such constructive-developmentally-oriented career counseling has been described elsewhere (McAuliffe, 1993). The classic career development activity aims at helping student counselors to "self-authorize" their career choices, to move from an external, conformist reliance on authority, to having one's own "vision of the work." So it goes with the graduate counseling student who would come to trust her own subjective "hunches" on the nature of a case and possible treatment plans. As she shares during this activity, her peer group affirms many of her hunches, either because they are shared or because the student has developed a creative contribution. Further, because of the importance of peer feedback to this activity, the authority of the professor, or the clinical supervisor, is shared, and thus a window may open to a constructivist epistemology.

What is described below incorporates classic case presentation strategies, as are used in internship and other clinical supervision. The twist lies in the group process of hearing and contributing to the case conceptualization. I have described elsewhere (McAuliffe, 1992) a variation on the common "S-O-A-P" model for presentation (See Appendix). In it, the presenter shares with the group four dimensions of an active case: the client's presenting concern and the counselor's reasons for bringing up the case ("Subjective"), information on the client based on the counselor's observation in the interview and any other data ("Objective"), a diagnostic impression ("Assessment"), and a treatment plan ("Plan").

This activity turns what is sometimes a pedestrian reporting of a case, with either an expert pronouncement by the clinical supervisor or an unstructured discussion by colleagues, into an event that honors subjectivity, intuition, and clinical expertise together. It can be especially empowering for the new practicum student, one who has been fed counseling theories and interviewing skills, but who must now exercise moment-to-moment judgment in sessions. It is an opportunity for self-authorizing through struggling to find and honor one's insights; it also relativizes knowledge as a social creation, in this case with a group of peers. Finally, it represents liberatory education (Freire, 1970) at its best, with the "teacher" becoming a "learner among adult learners."

Objectives

• To demonstrate the social construction of diagnosis and treatment planning

• To increase students' confidence in their own knowledge and insight

• To model a case presentation approach that might be used in group supervision on-site

Description of the Activity

In this "Go-Round" activity, the presenter (here called the "focus person") first prepares notes on the four SOAP dimensions prior to class. She or he then uses about ten minutes of class time to describe the first two SOAP dimensions. While she does so, the class members privately write their hunches, case conceptualizations, questions, ideas about themes, and any other impressions that are prompted by the focus person's story about the case. No comments or questions are allowed unless students find it crucial for clarifying "facts" (for example, "What was the client's age?").

After the presenter finishes sharing the first two SOAP dimensions, the class members share, one-by-one, an idea that is striking them. Each classmate gets a turn. The instructor has reminded them to be in "brainstorming" mode, to be aware of their hunches, to express ideas without evidence at this point. As each group member briefly shares their chosen idea, again, without description or justification, the presenter writes down <u>all</u> offerings, without editing or comment. She cannot respond at this time to questions, nor can she react to other hunches and ideas. "Just write" is the dictum.

Now begins the expansion, the conversation phase. The presenter reads aloud each offering and comments or asks for clarification. She might ask, "What did you mean by, 'I sense sexual abuse in this situation.'?" Or, "Let me respond to the question, 'Why did you refer for family counseling instead of seeing them yourself?'" This phase can last for up to ten minutes, with participants giving reasons for their hunches or listening to counter-perspectives from group members and/or the instructor.

When discussions about the first two SOAP dimensions have been exhausted, the presenter continues her recitation, based on the last two SOAP dimensions: her assessment, or diagnostic impression ("A") and her plan ("P"). After the plan is shared, students go through a similar process of brainstorming and naming their ideas for assessment and treatment plan. The presenter now has a fuller picture of issues to probe, dimensions to consider, and treatment modes to try.

Each member has participated on the "knowledge constructing team." Each has contributed her or his expertise, thus distributing the expertise beyond the instructor. The very notion of assessment and planning has become much more complex, as dimensions such as family, personal history, physical health, disabilities, system factors, alternate treatment theories, and client strengths have been considered as part of the mix. The group has contributed to the assessment the expertise of the diagnostic manual and/or the clinical supervisor take their place beside the expertise of each counselor. The essentialist fallacy is exposed, as members of the community see case conceptualization as a grand and continuing act of social construction.

It is worth noting that the instructor may propose her own ideas at any time. She needn't be shy about offering such. She is also a member of the community. She brings her particular experience and prior knowledge to the discussion. Even didactic instruction might have an occasional place, as novices often need skills training and modeling. However, it is our ultimate task as educators to create empowered professionals, to help our students see themselves as fellow knowledge creators. The group case go-round demonstrates the fluidity of evolving case conceptualizations. Through the go-round, students might see, for all time, that they have important ideas, that their "hunches" are good starting-places, that discussion of evidence often modifies such notions for the better, and that we can all have our ten minutes of fame as contributors to the clinical discourse.

REFERENCES

Freire, P. (1970). *Pedagogy of the oppressed.* New York: Continuum.

Haag-Granello. (1999). "Assessing the cognitive development of counseling students." Paper presented at the triennial meeting of the Association for Counselor Education and Supervision, New Orleans, LA.

McAuliffe, G. J. (1992). A case presentation approach to group supervision for community college counselors. *Counselor Education and Supervision, 31,* 163-174.

McAuliffe, G. J. (1993). Constructive development and career transition: Implications for counseling. *Journal of Counseling and Development, 72,* 23-28.

CASE STUDIES
—Gail Uellendahl and Joan Blacher

The case study method has historically been used to enhance critical thinking and active learning in the fields of business (McNair & Harsum, 1954) and public administration (Stillman, 1996). It has also been helpful in teaching medical diagnosis to doctors, classroom skills to teachers, and legal decision making to lawyers (McDade, 1988). More recently, counselor educators (Corey, 1996) and psychologists (Corsini & Wedding, 1995) have adopted the case study method. We find it useful in the practicum, consultation, and career development courses.

Case studies present a problem that requires clarification or resolution. The narrative typically specifies the facts of a situation, including those that led up to the problem, and describes the individual or individuals who are involved in the problem. The case may be real—disguised for confidentiality—or completely fictional. Usually, the case presents an individual or group facing a crossroad that requires a decision.

The case study method provokes problem solving and critical thinking by requiring learners to analyze the facts in the case, determine the important issues, and then make recommendations for improving or resolving the presented problem. During this analysis, learners not only add to their content knowledge about the topic illustrated by the case, but they actively engage themselves in collaborative learning.

From the constructivist, developmental teaching perspective, case study pedagogy promotes finding multiple methods and solutions, and supports student centered, developmental learning. For instance, case studies use participants' culture, experiences, frames of reference, and developmental levels to inform the direction and style of finding solutions. Case studies also reinforce the notion that there is no one "right" solution for problems and that knowledge is a "personal" matter (Rogers, 1983).

The instructor models tolerance for ambiguity as she/he challenges students to explore alternative solutions, particularly alternatives to those approaches that the instructor has endorsed; such tolerance is one of many characteristics of effective counselors (Blocher, 1966; Bordin, 1955; Brams, 1961; Jones, 1974). Educators also stimulate reflective thinking in their students, encouraging them to use self-awareness as a tool for further development, by asking students "how" they thought about and approached each case.

Description of the Activity

One of the difficulties faced by counselor educators who teach the theories course is providing learning experiences that clearly distinguish dif-

ferent theoretical approaches. Students often complain about their difficulties in discriminating among theories. The case study method provides
an excellent training vehicle with which to address this problem. Also, because working with cases requires students to apply various counseling
approaches, case studies provide a bridge between theory and practice.

   Writing cases. When we design cases for the Counseling Theory course,
for example, we describe the following elements:

1. the protagonist and his/her situation, including gender, age, marital
   and family status, work situation, personality, and social issues. (We
   write the case from the perspective of the protagonist.)

2. other individuals who are important to the problem, clearly defining
   their relationship to the protagonist.

3. significant background events.

4. a problem that is made relevant to the theoretical approach being studied.

5. a case with some complexities.

   Including complete information is not necessary; just as in real life, all
of the facts may not be available. Cases may be written either by the counselor educator, using the above guidelines, or by students in the class. If
the instructor writes cases, he/she intentionally illustrates specific theories, deliberately including challenging elements. If students write cases,
they bring their personal perspectives and possibly their own problem situations to the cases. Brown, Collins, and Duguid (1989) have shown that
personalizing learning in this way provides superior ground for learning.
It also promotes students' active participation in each phase of the learning process and reduces the damaging effects of power differentials.

   Writing study questions. We also provide a guide for analyzing cases.
The questions included in the guide reflect our learning objectives:

1. What are the important facts in the case?

2. What is the problem that the client brought to the counselor?

3. What would the (insert theory) approach say was the cause of the problem?

4. What decisions need to be made?

5. What are the conflicts?

6. What strategies would you use in working with the client?

7. Are there alternatives?

8. What would you hope might be some possible outcomes of counseling?

Changing the race, sexual orientation, gender, religion, or ethnicity of the client in the case after the students complete the initial process raises questions related to diversity and allows students to become aware of biases that may affect their counseling.

Sample case study 1. Carmen, an 18 year old, single female comes in for counseling. She has recently completed high school and lives at home with her mother and father, on whom she is quite dependent. She states that she feels both depressed and anxious. When you press for details you discover that she has many fears. She becomes particularly anxious when she must interact with others, especially strangers. Carmen currently works as a clerk in a retail store but has been offered a job in sales starting in September. She would like to take the job but is fearful about interacting with the public. She often berates herself for being such a "fraidy cat" and winds up feeling helpless and stupid.

Select a theoretical approach that you think might be useful in counseling this client. Answer the questions (see guide) in your discussion group.

Sample case study 2. You are a middle school counselor working in a diverse, urban setting. An eighth grader, Miguel, has been referred to you following numerous absences from school. His mother contacted the school for help in "keeping my son off the streets." Miguel has recently been seen with several members of one of the local gangs. His school record indicates that he achieved high grades through the seventh grade but has been performing poorly since last semester when his father died.

Considering the developmental tasks of adolescence, along with his history, what issues might you address with this student? What techniques/approaches would you employ? Are there other people with whom you might consult to help Miguel?

In-class procedures. We first distribute the sample case studies and the guide. We generally allow small groups to work on each case for fifteen to twenty minutes; we then discuss the case as a larger class. Once students share their analyses and reflections, the instructor demonstrates counseling strategies using the case. Later, as students develop more advanced skills, they use the case for role playing.

REFERENCES

Blocher, D. H. (1966). *Developmental counseling.* New York: Ronald Press.

Bordin, E. S. (1955). Ambiguity as a therapeutic variable. *Journal of Consulting Psychology, 19,* 9-15.

Brams, J. M. (1961). Counselor characteristics and effective communication in counseling. *Journal of Counseling Psychology, 8,* 25-30.

Brown, J. S., Collins, A. & Duguid, P. (1989). Situated cognition and the culture of learning. *Educational Researcher, 18* (1), 32-42.

Corey, G. (1996). *Theory and practice of counseling and psychotherapy* (5th ed.). Pacific Grove, CA: Brooks/Cole Publishing Company.

Corsini, R., & Wedding, D. (Eds.). (1995). *Current psychotherapies* (5th ed.). Itasca, IL: F. E. Peacock.

Jones, L. K. (1974). Toward more adequate selection criteria: Correlates of empathy, genuineness, and respect. *Counselor Education and Supervision, 14,* 13-17.

McDade, S. A. (1988). *An introduction to the case study method: Preparation, analysis, and participation.* Unpublished manuscript, Harvard College.

McNair, M. P., & Harsum, A. C. (1954). *The case method at the Harvard Business School.* New York: McGraw-Hill.

Rogers, C. (1983). *Freedom to learn in the 80's.* Columbus, OH: Merrill.

Stillman, R. J. (1996). *Public administration: Concepts and cases* (6th ed.). Boston: Houghton Mifflin Company.

7

Using Projects as Teaching Tools

Karen Eriksen

Since the 1920's, when Dewey implored teachers to engage students in topics that the students were interested in and that they could investigate on their own, project-based learning has had a central place in much schooling. However, with the exception of student presentations, project-based learning is sadly absent in the college classroom. Yet projects can powerfully impact students' sense of autonomy (a sense of themselves as creators and contributors), their sense of belonging (through connectedness to a peer group), and their sense of mastery, as they give up the "sponge" role for that of architect and builder. Projects have other of the same virtues as many "active learning" strategies—they are interesting, emotionally engaging, often of cooperative, and (can be) process-oriented.

Projects can consist of any of the following activities: research-and-oral presentation, observation and write-up ("ethnographies"), collecting information from surveys and/or interviews, and experiments. The last three are rarer, but especially valuable, as they put the student into a field setting to study phenomena first-hand. Like most active learning strategies, projects are time-consuming, although the time is mostly spent out of class. Below are two project activities, one a simulation of professional advocacy and the other community interviews followed by a class panel presentation. Both are planned and carried out by the students, with instructor guidance.   —*Garrett McAuliffe*

USING SIMULATION TO TEACH ABOUT PROFESSIONAL ASSOCIATIONS AND ADVOCACY

Counselors are often reluctant to engage in professional advocacy, or the promotion of their profession. Yet, leaders in the counseling field indicate that advocacy has been responsible for the significant gains that counselors have made in being able to practice what they were trained to do. Counseling leaders further suggest that counseling students be engaged as quickly as possible in this important process.

In the service of training students in advocacy, this exercise asks small groups of students to form a student counseling association and walk through Eriksen's (1997) seven stages of advocacy while working on an issue of importance to them. The simulation engages students actively in advocacy, and, by doing so, increases their retention of knowledge necessary for taking action on threats to the profession. Students alsoresearch and take on different organizational roles, which increases knowledge of professional association positions, specifically, and professional associations, more generally. Further, students participating in the simulation access multiple resources during the learning process, and incorporate the world of practice into their classroom learning experience. This helps them to anticipate real life situations and work out solutions before reaching an actual job situation. In addition, the project builds teamwork, collaboration, and cohesiveness among classmates, allows them to learn from each other, and brings past experiences to the learning process. It taps into the "right brain," stimulating their intuitive, creative, emotional, and spontaneous sides. Finally, this exercise empowers students with the sense that they can have an impact on their learning environments and their future professional environments.

Students may be initially reluctant to take part in an advocacy project, since advocacy is not the reason they are becoming counselors. A project also requires activities beyond the "easier" task of merely reading. However, students in my courses have chosen to invest many more hours in their projects than has been recommended due to the personal relevance of the projects that they have selected. Further, the students participating in projects such as these have often become the most active in the "real" student association and in advocating for counseling student benefits. Students in my courses have often gotten so excited about their ideas that they have presented them to the counseling program as a whole, and have been granted the opportunity to direct the incorporation of these ideas into the counseling program. It should be noted that a potential "political" problem may exist, however, in programs that are not ready for student advocacy, as after the simulations students may pressure programs to become more accountable.

While the advocacy project is probably best suited for the Internship Seminar or for the Introduction to the Profession of Counseling (professionalization) course, other types of simulations may be used in other courses. For instance, Colby and Long (1994) describe a mock trial that is useful in an ethics course. They bring in judges and lawyers from the community, use an issue pertinent to the profession (such as sexual misconduct by a counselor), and have the class prepare the background material for each of the simulation participants. Both Myer (2001) and Peterson & Myer, (1995) describe a Community Counseling course in which students develop a human service agency. For that project, small groups of students work together to choose the following: the type of agency; the type of clients served; the funding sources; how the program will be evaluated; how the program will be staffed; the basis of doing a needs assessment and literature search, and the types of programs and services to be offered. They prepare a budget and develop policies and procedures.

Objectives

- Students will become aware of the benefits and roles of professional associations .

- Students will learn how to advocate for themselves, their clients, and the profession.

Description of the Activity

Students begin the advocacy activity by reading Part One of Eriksen's (1997) *Making an Impact: A Handbook on Counselor Advocacy.* Part One clearly outlines the steps in an advocacy project, giving examples and rationales. Students then engage in a class exercise and perhaps a course-long project in which they apply the model presented in the book. During class, they divide into small groups, and receive the following handout (please note that each question has a corresponding exercise in the book):

———

You are forming a professional association, called the *Association of University Students of Counseling,* to address the needs you have as counseling students. In forming this association, you might want to consider the following:

- What needs do you have as counseling students that are not being addressed? (Problem identification)

- Who are you as students that decision-makers ought to attend to your concerns? (Identity)

- What would you like to do to address these unmet needs? Which are priorities?

- What resources are needed and what resources are you personally willing to commit? (Resource Assessment)

- Decide to take action on one priority. Make plans for background research to discover who may be currently working on this problem, and what information is currently available. Develop a time line for future action and meetings. (Strategic Planning)

- Decide on an organizational structure best suited for the action you have planned

- Take action. (Taking Action)

- Plan to evaluate your project and celebrate your successes

———

Each small group works on these questions during one class period, decides on their priorities, and makes plans for future action. They carry out the action plan outside of class during the remainder of the semester. The professor coaches the groups through the process, answering questions as they arise. As part of resource assessment and background research, students attend professional association meetings and talk with professional association leaders about how groups are organized and how they achieve their purposes. They may participate in the advocacy effort of a local professional association. Further, the professor helps students connect with on- and off- campus resources related to their particular issue.

Each group then presents the results of their simulation during a class period at the end of the semester, and passes out any related information they may have developed that would be helpful to the rest of the class. Projects undertaken by classes in the past have included:

- developing a mentoring program and package for incoming students;

- developing a student and alumni directory which listed interest areas, so that students could network and connect with practicing counselors with similar interests;

- putting on a conference for students that featured counselors from the community as speakers;

- planning a "Hill Day" in which a group of students visited the American Counseling Association headquarters for a briefing and then lobbied Congress on a counseling issue;

- forming a counseling student association in a university that didn't have one;

- forming an "improving teaching and curriculum" committee—this committee informed students who were unhappy with a class or a professor on procedures to follow in expressing their concerns; it supported the students in following these procedures; and advocated for more useful teacher selection and evaluation procedures.

REFERENCES

Colby, C. R., & Long, L. L. (1994). The use of a mock trial as an instructional method in counselor preparation. *Counselor Education and Supervision, 34*(1), 58-67.

Eriksen, K. P. (1997). *Making an impact: A handbook on counselor advocacy.* Muncie, IN: Accelerated Development.

Myer, R. (2001). Community agency counseling: Teaching about management and administration. In K. Eriksen and G. McAuliffe, *Teaching counselors and therapists,* (pp. 355-370). Westport, CT: Bergin & Garvey.

Peterson, S. E., & Myer, R. A. (1995). The use of collaborative project-based learning in counselor education. *Counselor Education and Supervision, 35* (2), 150-158.

THE COMMUNITY INTERVIEW AND
PANEL DISCUSSION ACTIVITY

Adult education writers indicate that students should be immersed in relevant employment settings from the beginnings of their programs in order to reduce the gap between theory and practice. Yet, educators themselves often lack such experiences or have not been in the field for many years. Students and others frequently complain that academics live in an ivory tower away from the world of practice. They worry that such academics may not be able to convey the current realities of a professional workplace. One way of addressing the need for real-world knowledge in counselor preparation programs might be to have students conduct Community Interviews and Panel Discussions.

In this activity, students interview members of special population groups, read an article on counseling that particular group, and present their findings to peers as part of a panel. In the process, they encounter the varying experiences of their co-panelists who report on the same population group. The dialogue following presentation of these contrasting perspectives encourages both co-construction of knowledge and respect for different perspectives.

Students experience many benefits from this exercise. They find the panel presentation format a fun and entertaining way to learn. Their retention increases as a result of taking some action during learning, organizing their own thoughts about the experience, and teaching others what they have learned. Interviewing allows them to learn about people firsthand, which adds color, depth, and emotion to the material they encounter when reading books and articles. Further, interviewing encourages students to access a greater variety of resources and become less dependent on the "authority" of the professor or the textbook. Also, students can interview representatives of those population groups with whom they may work in the future, allowing them to make the assignment personally and professionally relevant. Finally, while I had not initially planned this as a learning objective, students were often surprised at their own positive reactions to people different than themselves, people who might have problems they had never encountered. They found themselves less afraid of and, in turn, less willing to create distance between themselves and members of the groups they had interviewed. Many became volunteers in human service agencies and some resolved to treat homeless people on the street with greater kindness.

Community Interviews and Panel Discussions are applicable to many different courses, although if several instructors in the same program are using this activity, coordination is necessary to prevent unnecessary repetition for students. I have used it in the Introduction to Counseling and the Community Counseling courses as a means to survey the population groups counselors are likely to encounter in their future job settings. Students could also interview employees at different human services agencies or people holding the job positions to which they aspire. In Multicultural Counseling or Counseling Special Populations courses, students might interview people from cultures or groups other than their own. In the Human Growth and Development course, students could interview people at different developmental levels, either different age levels, moral development levels, or cognitive development levels. In a Family Therapy course, students might interview members of different types of families. In Addictions courses, students could interview people addicted to different substances. And in Diagnosis and Treatment Planning courses, students might interview people with varying diagnoses. (Clearly ethical concerns about interviews with these people would need to be discussed; however, it has been my experience that students know people in the community with many of the DSM IV diagnoses.)

Objectives

- Students will actively encounter people in the community who are different from themselves, people who they are likely to encounter in their future employment settings.

- They will decrease their fears of those who are different, decrease the "us-them" distance, and find ways to fit new perspectives into their current ways of perceiving clients and counseling.

- Further, students will encounter and become more open to multiple perspectives when they hear the differing results of their peers' interviews with people from the same population groups.

- Finally, class members will encounter some information on a wide range of prospective client groups.

Description of the Activity

During the first class period, the instructor lists the population groups to be studied during the semester (for example, gay, lesbian, or transgendered people; people of various races or ethnicities; people of various ages; men and women; people with physical disabilities; and people with alcohol or drug problems). Students sign up to conduct interviews with members of two or three of these groups. At least three students sign up to interview representatives from the same population group. A key to the success of this exercise is ensuring that some of those interviewed are not "clinically" disturbed.

The instructor develops an interview format, such as one of those presented in Neukrug's book (1994, pp. 288-290) and demonstrates to the class how to conduct such an interview. When interviewing a gay person, for instance, questions might include, "What would you like counselors to know about what it is like to be gay?" "What are some of the advantages of being gay?" "What are some of the greatest challenges about being gay?" "If you pursued counseling, what would you want your counselor to know about gay people?"

Students then spend approximately one hour interviewing a representative from one of the population groups, getting to know him or her, and discovering how counselors might provide effective services to this group of people. The students also assess their own comfort, discomfort, or counter-transference issues related to working with people from this population group. Students may be asked to read an article on counseling this population group or to find several resources specific to meeting the needs of this population group. Finally, students prepare a two-page handout about their discoveries for their classmates.

During the class session that follows the interviews, the students who interviewed members of the same population group form a panel at a front table facing the rest of the class. They take turns presenting key elements of what they learned; they distribute a summary in a handout. The instructor serves as panel moderator and encourages panel members and class members to discuss any differences or similarities between the panel members' discoveries. Questions might include, "What differences and similarities do you hear among the panel members' reports?" "Where do you think the differences come from?" "What do these differences tell you about the 'clients'?" "About the panelists?" "What key learning will you take with you into your practice as a counselor?"

After all the panels have presented (which may take several class periods), the instructor leads a closing discussion about what students learned during the activity. The professor might suggest journaling about the activity as another way for students to explore and reflect on their experience.

REFERENCE

Neukrug, E. (1994). *Theory, practice, and trends in human services.* Pacific Grove, CA: Brooks/Cole.

Index

About the Editors and Contributors

Lois Benishek is an assistant professor and Director of the Master's in Counseling Psychology Program at Temple University. Her research interests focus on positive adjustment and resilience, as well as professional development issues as they pertain to under-represented populations in academe. She is currently on the editorial board for *The Journal of Counseling & Development* and is actively involved in both the Association for Women in Psychology (AWP) and APA's Division 17 Counseling Psychology's Section for the Advancement of Women.

Joan Blacher is Professor Emerita, School of Education, California Lutheran University, where she served as the Director of the Counseling and Guidance program for eleven years. Prior to her university affiliation, Dr. Blacher was a counselor, school psychologist and administrator in the public schools. In private practice as a marriage and family therapist for the past 16 years, she specializes in family and career transitions. She has served as President of the California Association of Counselor Educators and Supervisors and the Ventura County Association of School Psychologists, and is currently a member of the California Association for Counseling and Development Journal Editorial Board. Her research interests include career counseling and counselor's use of assessment.

Raquel Contreras is the Director of Psychological Services for the International Pain Institute at the Texas Tech University Health Sciences Center. She is also an Assistant Professor for the Department of Anesthesiology. Prior to this appointment, she was the Director of Training for the Internship Program at the Texas Tech University Counseling Center. Areas of interest include: training issues, multiculturalism, and chronic pain.

Karen Eriksen teaches counseling at Radford University and is licensed as a Professional Counselor and Marriage and Family Counselor in Virginia. She spent 18 years as a mental health and community agency counselor, gaining specialties in family therapy, addictions, survivors of sexual abuse, and the intersection of spirituality and counseling. Dr. Eriksen is a Nationally Certified Counselor, an AAMFT Clinical Member, and an AAMFT Approved Supervisor. She has written the only book on the process of professional advocacy—*Making an Impact: A Handbook on Counselor Advocacy*. She has co-authored *Preparing Counselors and Therapists: Creating Constructivist and Developmental Programs*. Her research areas are in counselor advocacy and counselor preparation. Active in leadership of several state and national professional associations, including: ACA, VAMFC, VACC, AMHCA, VCA, NVCCC, and IAMFC, she is currently President-elect of VAMFC. She presents workshops on advocacy and counselor preparation at local, state, and national conferences.

Nathalie Kees is an associate professor of Counseling and Career Development in the School of Education at Colorado State University and has been a counselor educator for 14 years. Dr. Kees served as guest editor for the Journal for Specialists in Group Work's special issue on Women's Groups and is currently serving as chair for the ACA Task Force on Women in Counseling. She is a current editorial board member of JCD. Her research interests include the spirituality of education, women's issues, and group work.

William M. Kurtines is professor of psychology and Director of the Doctoral Program in Developmental Psychology in the Department of Psychology at Florida International University. Professor Kurtines has been a visiting faculty member in the Department of Psychology at University of Texas at Austin, in the School of Education at Harvard University, and a Visiting Scientist at the Max Planck Institute for Education and Human Development in Berlin, Germany. Dr. Kurtines' areas of scholarly and research interest include social and personality development, family development, life span developmental psychology, cross cultural psychology, and moral development.

Rolla E. Lewis is an assistant professor and coordinator of the school counseling specialization at Portland State University. Dr. Lewis has taught, led groups, and counseled students in alternative and public school settings for over fifteen years. He is past president of the Oregon Association for Counselor Education and Supervision and author of a number of book chapters and articles. His current research interests focus on fostering resiliency and using structured narratives to foster positive transitions.

Aretha Faye Marbley is an assistant professor in Counselor Education at Texas Tech University, and chapter president for the National Coalition of 100 Black Women. She has presented locally, nationally, and internationally and published in the area of social support systems within marginalized family and community structures. Recently, she was invited to give expert testimony to the Committee on Criminal Jurisprudence of the Texas House of Representatives.

Garrett McAuliffe is the Graduate Program Director of the nationally accredited counseling program at Old Dominion University. His current work focuses on cultural diversity, especially ethnicity, social class, and sexual orientation. He has trained college faculty on cultural sensitivity at a number of forums, and has a strong interest in adult cognitive development, especially as it affects moral choices and organizations, and college student change. He has published three books on the topic of constructivism and counselor education. Recognized by receiving the Tonelson Award for Outstanding Teaching in the Darden College of Education, he was also selected as one of eight Old Dominion Faculty members nominated for the Virginia Outstanding Faculty Award, known as the SCHEV Award.

James McGraw has twenty years of counseling experience in a variety of settings, including community mental health, correctional, in-patient psychiatric, and college counseling centers. Currently he is a counselor at Longview Community College and an adjunct faculty member at Webster University-Kansas City, teaching theory, research, and practica. He co-authored the book, *Essentials of Family Therapy: A Therapist's Guide to Eight Approaches.*

Marilyn J. Montgomery is an assistant professor of Psychology at Florida International University in Miami, Florida, where she is also the Practicum Coordinator for the Mental Health Research and Services Program. Her areas of interest include counselor development, diversity training for non-majority groups and individuals, and interventions that promote relationship enhancement through emotional development in families and small groups. Her most recent book is titled *Building Bridges to Parents.*

Michael O'Connor is an associate professor and former chair of the Department of Counseling and School Psychology at Seattle University. His post-doctorate studies include a Master's degree in Spirituality and Spiritual Direction. His professional interests are integrating spirituality into counseling and therapy, and teaching in other countries including England, Ireland, New Zealand, Nepal and Bhutan. He presents regularly on spiritual dimensions of counseling at ACA World Conferences, and at regional

ACES and state counseling association meetings.

Gail Uellendahl is currently is an associate professor and Director of the Counseling and Guidance Program at California Lutheran University. Prior to this position, she worked in the college student personnel field where she directed services for students with disabilities at Queens College of the City University of New York. She is a grant writer and her research interests include the use of assessment by school counselors, the nature of site supervision for masters level interns, and psychologists' knowledge and use of alternative treatment modalities. She is a licensed psychologist and maintains a private practice in Santa Monica.

Carlotta J. Willis is a licensed psychologist, certified Laban Movement Analyst, certified Psychomotor Therapist (Espenak), Nationally Certified Counselor, and Approved Clinical Supervisor (NBCC). She is interested in the role of nonverbal communication in counseling and creative approaches to career development. She is president of the North Atlantic Regional Association for Counselor Education and Supervision.